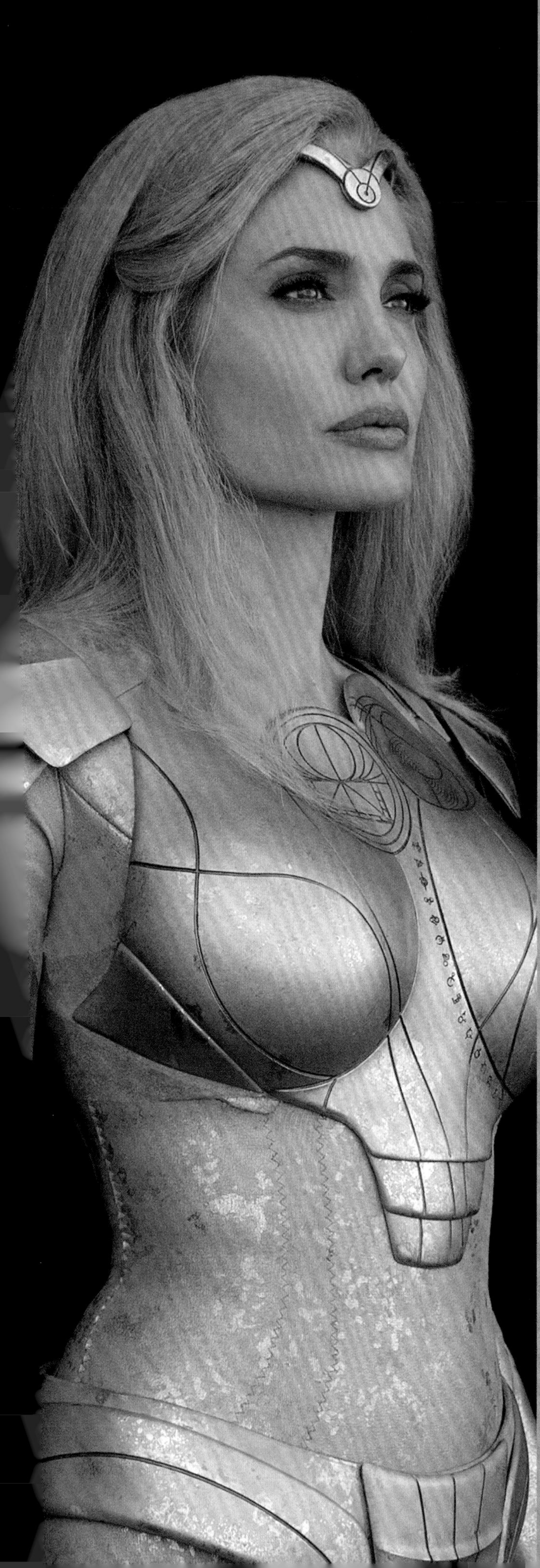

IN THIS ISSUE

DISNEY PUBLISHING WORLDWIDE
Global Magazines, Comics and Partworks

Publisher
Lynn Waggoner

Editorial Director
Bianca Coletti

Editorial Team
Guido Frazzini (Director, Comics), Stefano Ambrosio (Executive Editor, New IP), Carlotta Quattrocolo (Executive Editor, Franchise), Camilla Vedove (Senior Manager, Editorial Development), Behnoosh Khalili (Senior Editor), Julie Dorris (Senior Editor), Mina Riazi (Assistant Editor), Gabriela Capasso (Assistant Editor)

Design
Enrico Soave (Senior Designer)

Art
Ken Shue (VP, Global Art), Roberto Santillo (Creative Director), Marco Ghiglione (Creative Manager), Manny Mederos (Creative Manager), Stefano Attardi (Illustration Manager)

Portfolio Management
Olivia Ciancarelli (Director)

Business & Marketing
Mariantonietta Galla (Senior Manager, Franchise), Virpi Korhonen (Editorial Manager)

Text
Steve Behling

Graphic Design and Editing
Zampediverse

Contributor
Giulia Vielmi

Thanks to
Sarah Beers
Adam Davis
Keilah Jordan
Kyle Quigley
Erika Denton
Jeff Willis
Vincent Garcia

TITAN EDITORIAL
Editor Jonathan Wilkins
Group Editor Jake Devine
Art Director Oz Browne
Production Controller Kelly Fenlon
Production Controller Caterina Falqui
Production Manager Jackie Flook
Sales and Circulation Manager Steve Tothill
Marketing Coordinator Lauren Noding
Publicist Will O'Mullane
Digital and Marketing Manager Jo Teather
Acquisitions Editor Duncan Baizley
Publishing Directors Ricky Claydon & John Dziewiatkowski
Operations Director Leigh Baulch
Publishers Vivian Cheung & Nick Landau

DISTRIBUTION
U.S. Newsstand: Total Publisher Services, Inc.
John Dziewiatkowski, 630-851-7683
U.S. Distribution: Ingrams Periodicals, Curtis Circulation Company
U.K. Newsstand: Marketforce, 0203 787 9199
U.S./U.K. Direct Sales Market: Diamond Comic Distributors
For more info on advertising contact adinfo@titanemail.com

First edition August 2022

Marvel Studios' Eternals: The Official Movie Special is published by Titan Magazines, a division of Titan Publishing Group Limited, 144 Southwark Street, London SE1 0UP

Printed in China

For sale in the U.S., and Canada

ISBN: 9781787734678

Titan Authorized User. TMN 3671

A CIP catalogue record for this title is available from the British Library.

10 9 8 7 6 5 4 3 2 1

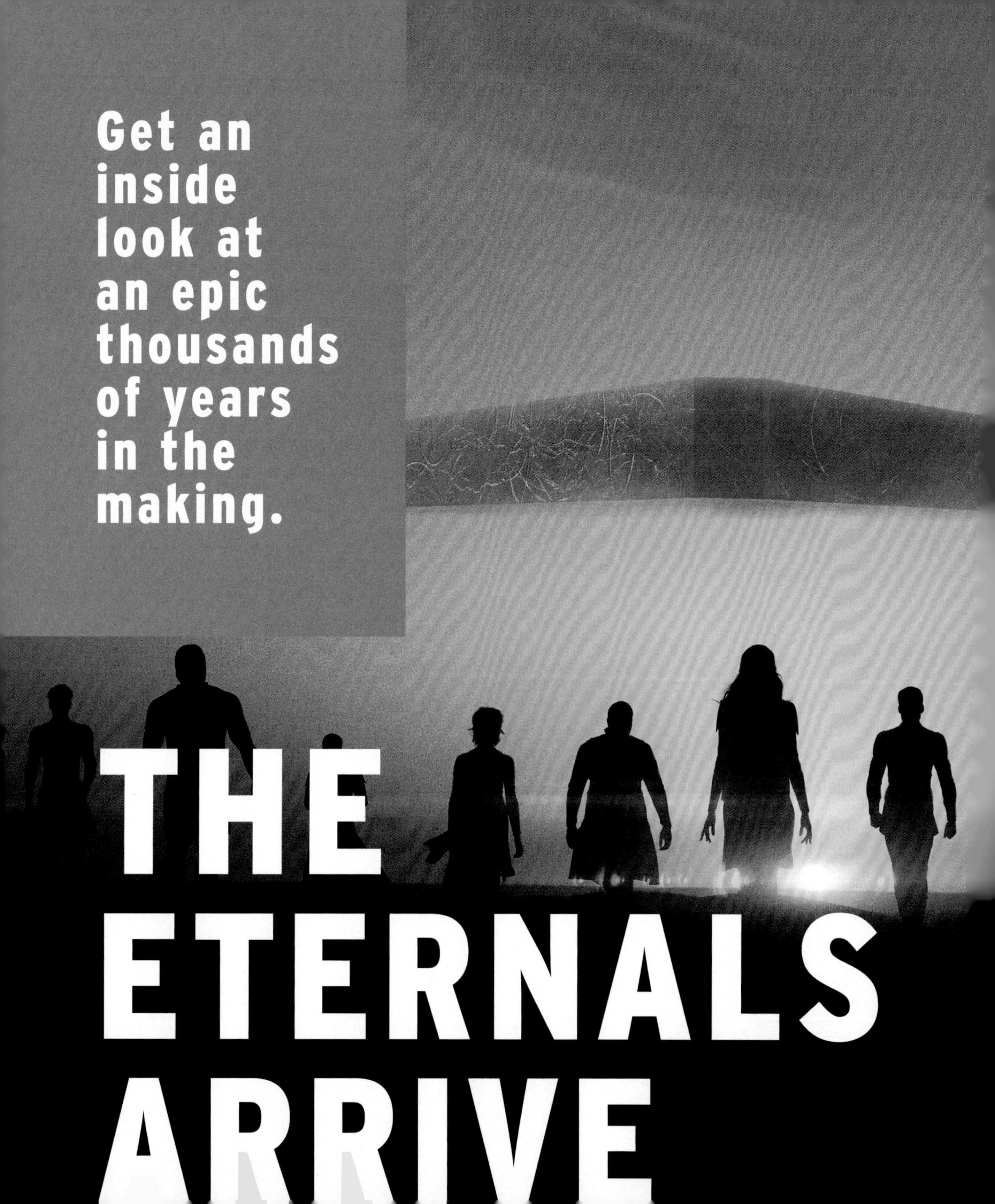

Get an inside look at an epic thousands of years in the making.

THE ETERNALS ARRIVE

Fans of the Marvel Cinematic Universe have seen the origins of such heroes as Iron Man and Captain America, witnessed the coming together of the Guardians of the Galaxy, and thrilled to the assembling of an incredible group of Super Heroes to thwart the twisted dreams of Thanos.

But now it's time to go back to the beginning of the Marvel Cinematic Universe itself, and watch with awe as *Marvel Studios' Eternals* takes center stage. This film spans thousands of years, from the time the Celestials sent the Eternals to Earth, until present day, when a terrifying threat from their past returns to wreak havoc anew. This is perhaps the most epic film that the Marvel Cinematic Universe has created so far, and not only for the chronological width of its story. *Marvel Studios' Eternals* deals with profound themes, such as the relationship between humanity and the divine and a love story that goes beyond millennia.

Inside, you'll learn more about the story of the film, meet the Eternals, delve into interviews with the cast and crew, and get a behind-the-scenes glimpse at the making of the movie. Then, you'll immerse yourself in an all-new comics adventure starring the Eternals. Now turn the page, and experience the unbelievable!

ABOVE: APPEARANCE OF A CELESTIAL.

Enter the world of the Eternals, as they face their greatest threat ever.

THE IMMORTAL STORY BEGINS

Almost everyone in the world of the Marvel Cinematic Universe knows who the Avengers are. But, while they might be able to rattle off the names of Earth's Mightiest Heroes, the unsuspecting people of Earth are unaware that another group of super beings has been on this planet for thousands of years. They are the Eternals, a group of ten sent to Earth by the Celestials over 7,000 years ago.

They were tasked to watch over the planet and quietly guide humanity in its growth and development from the shadows until the people of Earth are able to protect themselves. Led by the spiritual leader Ajak and their tactical leader, Ikaris, the Eternals consist of Thena, Sersi, Phastos, Sprite, Kingo, Gilgamesh, Makkari, and Druig. (To find out more about them, including their astounding abilities, turn to the "Who's Who — Heroes" section on page 6.) And if all the Eternals had to do was keep humanity moving in the right direction, they would still face a superhuman task. However, an ancient enemy has also arrived on Earth in the form of the Deviants. Frightening, predatory creatures that can assume the physical characteristics of their prey, the Deviants are a clear and present danger that must be stopped at any cost.

As years turn to decades, decades turn to centuries, and centuries turn into millennia, the immortal Eternals drift apart. The tight-knit team has scattered across the globe. And when a new Deviant threat arises, it falls upon Sersi and Ikaris to gather the members of their extended family to deal with it.

ABOVE: THE ETERNALS' SHIP ARRIVING ON EARTH.

Discover the heroes of *Marvel Studios' Eternals*.

WHO'S WHO HEROES

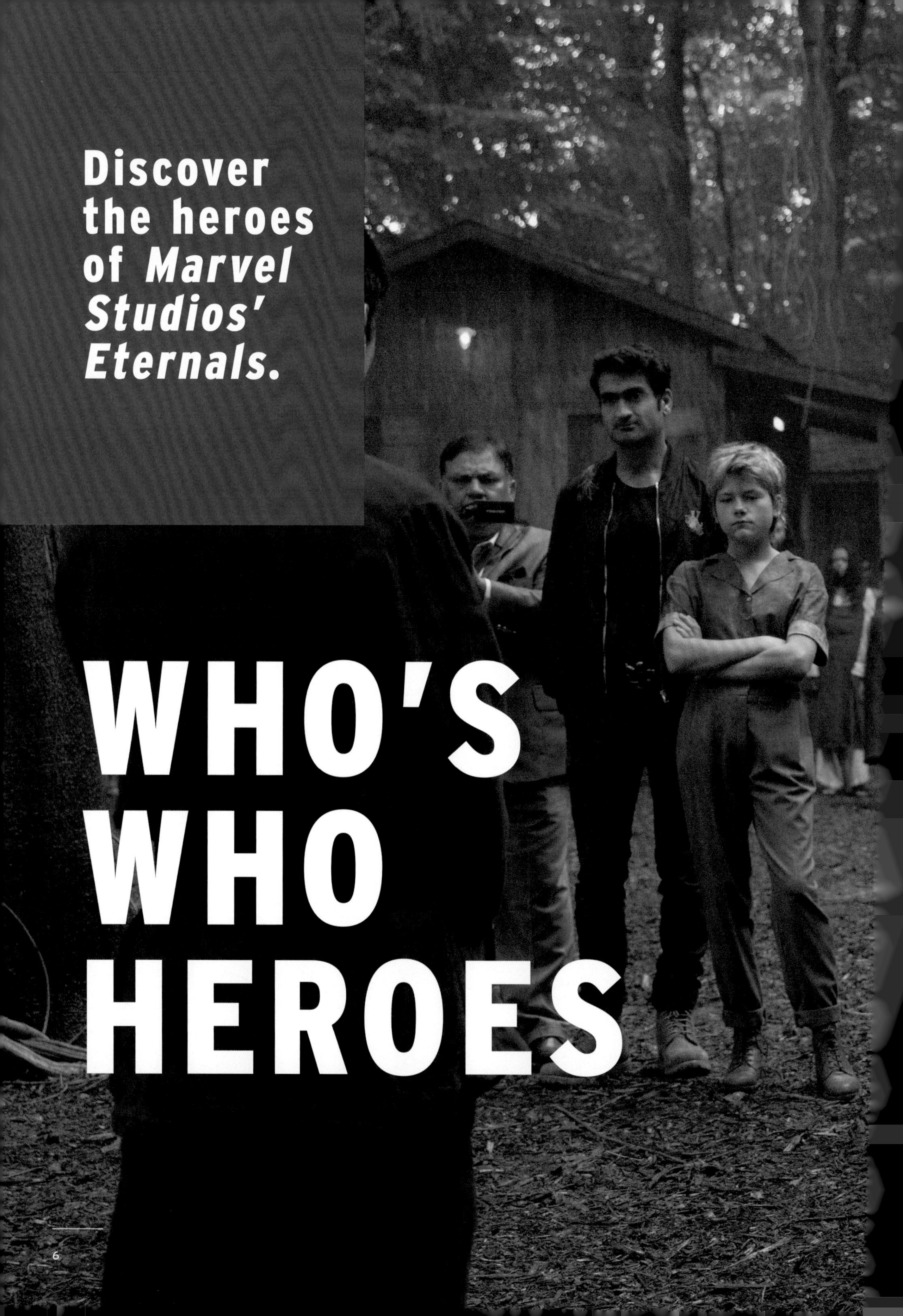

IKARIS

PORTRAYED BY

Richard Madden

ABILITIES

Super strength, flight, beam projection of cosmic energy from his eyes

BACKGROUND

Ikaris is the leader of the Eternals. Possessed of incredible strength, Ikaris alone among the Eternals also has the power of flight. He has been the team's tactical leader since their arrival on Earth over 7,000 years ago. Tasked by Ajak and the Celestials to inspire greatness across the universe, particularly on Earth, Ikaris has used his astounding abilities for the betterment of people the world over. He also has been madly in love with fellow Eternal Sersi, though their relationship, like any, has had ups and downs. In present day, Ikaris and Sersi are no longer together, though he still has feelings for her.

SERSI

PORTRAYED BY

Gemma Chan

ABILITIES

Matter transmutation

BACKGROUND

A strong woman with bright, curious eyes, Sersi has the ability to transmute matter from one form to another. In the blink of an eye, she can transform an out-of-control bus into flower petals, preventing it from crashing into a crowd of innocent bystanders. As the Eternals adjust themselves to their separate lives in the present-day world, Sersi has taken a job at a museum, where she works as a scientist alongside Dane Whitman. Sersi has feelings for Dane, yet finds herself in conflict when Ikaris reappears, and the Eternals must come together once more.

THENA

PORTRAYED BY

Angelina Jolie

ABILITIES

Manipulation of cosmic energy to create weapons

BACKGROUND

A highly skilled fighter with the ability to create weapons made of pure energy, Thena loves nothing more than to enter the fray. From the moment the Eternals arrived on Earth, Thena has used her powers to aid humans and defend them from the Deviants that would do them harm. Over the course of thousands of years, Thena has begun to slowly succumb to what the Eternals refer to as the Mahd Wy'ry — where the mind begins to fracture under the weight of countless memories. As the Eternals regroup in present day, Thena finds herself fighting this internal battle as well.

AJAK

PORTRAYED BY

Salma Hayek

ABILITIES

Healing power

BACKGROUND

The Eternal named Ajak is the spiritual leader of the group. She is the one who communicates with the Celestial Arishem, and gives the Eternals their missions. With the ability to heal anything she touches, Ajak has perhaps the most nurturing abilities of any Eternal. She knows that it isn't the Eternals' job to give humans answers to all their problems; rather, they must support the people of Earth so they may arrive at the answers themselves. Whether Ajak will be able to use her healing powers to help Thena and the Eternals in their renewed battle against the Deviants remains to be seen.

MAKKARI

GILGAMESH

PORTRAYED BY

Lauren Ridloff

ABILITIES

Super speed

BACKGROUND

Gifted with super speed, the Eternal known as Makkari can move with such velocity that she becomes a blur. She can even use that ability to speed-read, and can absorb vast amounts of information that way. Makkari is deaf, and communicates with her teammates via American Sign Language. Makkari is close to her teammates, and her incredible speed is often called upon when defending Earth against the Deviants or helping the humans to become their best selves. A speedster who never shies away from a fight, Makkari is a levelheaded hero who loves to read and collect relics.

PORTRAYED BY

Don Lee

ABILITIES

Super strength, cosmic exo-skeleton

BACKGROUND

An Eternal with astounding strength, Gilgamesh is a fighter through and through. Thanks to a "cosmic exo-skeleton," Gilgamesh is able to harness such strength as to cause shock waves when he throws a punch. He's capable of lifting boulders that weigh several tons. And yet, Gilgamesh is not a super serious, brooding hero. He enjoys himself, and life — something the other Eternals value. Acting as sort of a big brother to his teammates, Gilgamesh is especially protective of Thena, and would do anything to ensure her safety.

PHASTOS

PORTRAYED BY

Brian Tyree Henry

ABILITIES

Technology expert

BACKGROUND

Though he can certainly take care of himself and his fellow Eternals in a fight against the Deviants, Phastos is also the scientist of the group. A wizard with technology, he has used that ability for the betterment of humanity across thousands of years. Phastos has mastered all kinds of useful innovations to help the Eternals, such as the transport discs that carry the team from their ship, the Domo, to the Earth's surface. Phastos had shown great hope for all humanity through the millennia, but at some point, he seemed to abandon that hope. Will it be restored as he rejoins his family?

DRUIG

PORTRAYED BY

Barry Keoghan

ABILITIES

Mind control

BACKGROUND

Not all the Eternals have powers that are immediately noticeable. Take Druig, for example. He has the ability to control the minds of others. In the past, he has used this ability to quell conflicts on Earth, getting people to calm down and admit the error of their ways. He attempts to take violence out of the equation whenever possible — and yet, as the Eternals have obviously discovered from their time on Earth, it isn't always possible. Druig isn't supposed to directly interfere with humans, but there are times when even an Eternal can't help himself.

SPRITE

PORTRAYED BY

Lia McHugh

ABILITIES

Cast illusions

BACKGROUND

By all outward appearances the youngest Eternal (she appears to be a child), Sprite has also been alive for thousands upon thousands of years, like her teammates. Sprite has the unique ability to cast illusions, to create incredibly lifelike images. Over the millennia, Sprite has used her power to tell stories — she believes in the power of storytelling, and might also be responsible for gifting that capacity for stories to the people of Earth, too. Sprite can be a bit cheeky (she loves to tease her fellow Eternals), but would do anything for her family.

KINGO

PORTRAYED BY

Kumail Nanjiani

ABILITIES

Cosmic energy projection

BACKGROUND

Kingo has the ability to project blasts of ultra-powerful cosmic energy from his hands. He wields this power to aid the people of Earth, and fight against the Deviants that would overwhelm the planet. Though he misses his home planet of Olympia, Kingo has adapted to life on Earth. In fact, Kingo has adapted so well that he has, in present day, become a huge movie star in India, where he makes Bollywood films! He enjoys being famous, and the life that goes with being a celebrity. But he must choose between that life and helping his fellow Eternals when the Deviants return.

ANGELINA JOLIE AS THENA
WIELDING POWERS.

Meet the creatures who threaten to destroy Earth.

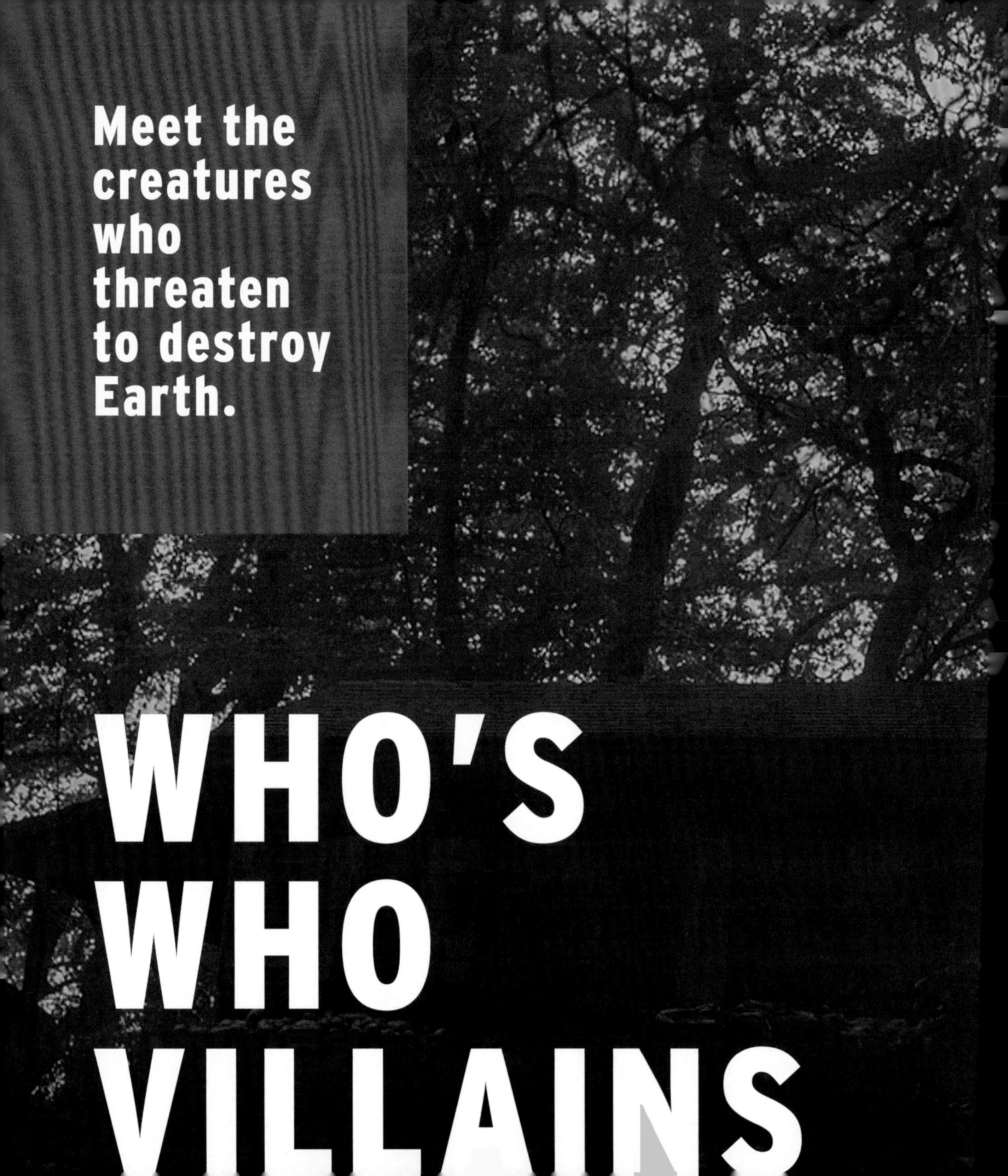

WHO'S WHO VILLAINS

According to Matthew and Ryan Firpo, two of the screenwriters on *Eternals*, the Deviants are the most ancient enemy on planet Earth. The Deviants "are twisted monsters that inspire all of early mankind's myths," says Matthew Firpo. "They're monsters, they're demons, all of our nightmares were sort of inspired by these creatures. Cave paintings of monsters? Those were Deviants."

The Deviants are among the first creatures ever to inhabit Earth, parasitic life forms that has been preying upon humans throughout history. It was only when the Eternals arrived on Earth, and fought the Deviants, that humans were at last able to advance.

As the centuries passed, the Deviants seemed to be a threat no longer. But recent events — and the appearance of a Deviant named Kro — proves that the world still needs the Eternals.

TOP: A CLOSE UP OF KRO.
ABOVE: ETERNALS FIGHTING DEVIANT WITH BLUE CASTLE IN BACKGROUND.

TOP: DEVIANT MENACING EARLY HUMANS.
ABOVE: KRO TAKES A PRISONER.

IKARIS IN TROUBLE AS THE DEVIANTS ATTACK.

We talked with director Chloé Zhao about the philosophy behind the film, the epic love story, and the history of Earth!

ETERNAL QUESTIONS

"We're tapping into a lot of philosophical questions about who we are. We're exploring that by traveling through time and following a really, really deeply beautiful, epic love story."

How has it been working with the Marvel Studios team to develop this film?
Chloé Zhao: Everyone has been super supportive. To be able to let your imagination just be set free and then to have people who are so experienced and open-minded to be able to take your ideas and elevate them is an incredible process. I'm learning. I'm just so excited.

What made you want to be a part of this project?
CZ: I've always been a fan of the Marvel Cinematic Universe. I've seen all the films. And I just fell deeply in love with the characters. When I read about this story, I was drawn to how colorful and truly diverse these characters are. And the questions that are asked in this film are the most humanistic questions — questions that I ask as a human being, a mortal. So, it is going to be a very entertaining and beautiful film. But it's also a very thoughtful and a very humanistic one. That's what really excites me.

We're tapping into a lot of philosophical questions about who we are. We're exploring that by traveling through time and following a really, really deeply beautiful, epic love story. And, at the same time, asking questions about who we are as human beings on this planet. And I think that's everything we love about a great piece of humanistic storytelling like Marvel has always done.

What do we learn about the origins of the Marvel Cinematic Universe from this film?
CZ: [In past films] we've seen what's in space and what's on Earth coming together. And usually, those two things are in conflict. But what I love about *Eternals* is how we learn that, actually, what's out there and what's on Earth have been evolving together from the very beginning of time. And these Eternals have been helping us shape our history and who we are. And we also have shaped who they are — the choices humanity made had a great effect on them as well. So, we're not that different. We've been learning from each other and co-existing for all this time. And I think that has changed how we look at some of the heroes [in the MCU] we've met so far.

What would you say sets Eternals *apart from other Marvel films?*
CZ: First of all, we go back into history, at the beginning of time for this planet [Earth]. We explore a lot of mythology we haven't seen yet. And at the core of this film is an epic love story.

Who are the Eternals?
CZ: They were sent by the Celestials. They were sent to protect this planet but, also, to help humanity advance and become rulers of this planet themselves. There was a time when we looked at Eternals as gods. And, at some point in human history, we went from worshipping gods and super humans to worshipping human beings as heroes. We went from theism to humanism. That's when humanity started to be able to protect themselves — you know, we have the Avengers. So where do Eternals belong in today's world? The film very much explores their journey to figure that out.

Can you tell us anything about the Deviants?
CZ: Our villains are the Deviants. And they are much scarier, I think, than any monsters we've met so far. We wanted to go into a lot of mythology in human history and be inspired by monsters from different cultures. We're basically implying that [these monsters] were created in these artworks and stories because the Deviants had been here. They are, essentially, space parasites. They're powerful enough to inhabit a planet and destroy everything that's alive.

ANGELINA JOLIE AND CHLOÉ ZHAO HAVING FUN BEHIND THE SCENES.

Could you talk about the characters Ikaris and Sersi?
CZ: Sersi is a very creative person. I think what excites me about her character is that she doesn't really punch anybody. Her power comes from her curiosity, her ability to connect with sentient and non-sentient beings, to reshape them. She's an artist, a creative person. And she has a deep connection to nature. She's curious about humanity in a way that other Eternals might not be. And she's curious about what it means to live a transient life that doesn't last forever. That's not her own. Her compassion comes out of that curiosity, and is what makes her a really powerful Super Hero.

And Ikaris is your ultimate Super Hero.
CZ: I think they look at humanity very differently. One analogy I really like is that when Ikaris sees a desert, Sersi sees grains of sand. And she finds beauty and miracles in every grain of sand. But Ikaris doesn't really see that, because he's the tactical leader of the Eternals. He has bigger issues he's dealing with. He's looking at, "Okay, now, there's danger in the desert. We need to go." But Sersi is focusing on what each tiny molecule means, each life matters.

They are not together when we first meet them in present day [in this movie]. But they're brought together by a situation they have to deal with. And they're trying to learn how they could come back together again.
I don't think they ever fell out of love. I think they're soul mates.

What does it mean to be an Eternal?
CZ: To live forever is a blessing and a curse. We go on these emotional journeys with these Eternals to figure out who they are. And, strangely enough, the film actually becomes very much of a celebration of planet Earth and a celebration of humanity.

But, by going through this journey with them to try to figure out who they are, we are learning about what it means to be mortal as well. And, therefore, we're learning what it means to be a human being that has a very limited amount of time in this universe to exist. We feel certain things the Eternals are yearning to feel. And Sersi, specifically, as a character, is trying to understand how she could feel and look at the world through a human being's perspective who only has a limited amount of time. And I think that's a beautiful way to celebrate humanity.

ABOVE: KEVIN FEIGE (PRODUCER) AND VICTORIA ALONSO (EXECUTIVE PRODUCER) WITH CHLOÉ ZHAO.

We got some insight about Sersi from Gemma Chan, and talked about the film's diverse cast, as well as balancing character and action.

SERSI SPEAKS

"Our story is very much about these characters and how they feel about each other and how they feel about the world."

What's it like entering this phase of the Marvel Cinematic Universe?
Gemma Chan: Well, first of all, I should say I feel very lucky to be in the Marvel Cinematic Universe. Being part of this new phase and a new group of characters is quite exciting. And I think this film is trying to do something a little bit different than what has come before.

Can you introduce us to your character, Sersi?
GC: Sersi is an Eternal, she's an empath, and she can manipulate matter. So, she can turn things into other things. Sersi doesn't quite understand the extent of her powers the first time you meet her in the film. Only over time, she discovers that she is more powerful than she ever thought.

What can you tell us about the story?
GC: The Eternals have been on Earth for the last 7,000 years. And for a fair bit of that time they've been in hiding, living amongst humans or in exile. They first came to Earth to protect humans from the Deviants, to allow humankind to evolve and to develop, for civilizations to grow as they have done to the present day. And they think they've eliminated all the Deviants, and the Eternals have been waiting to be called home at the start of the film.

This is a big film. Can you talk for a moment about what it's like balancing delicate character moments with Super Hero action?
GC: I think it's a tricky balance. But I think that's what's great about [Marvel Studios] films — you have big spectacle, these huge set pieces, but you also have really quiet, character-driven moments. Heartfelt moments between two people who are just trying to connect. Or, there are funny moments. There are very sad moments. And really, that's what glues the whole thing together. Our story is very much about these characters and how they feel about each other and how they feel about the world. And that's what drives the narrative.

ABOVE: GEMMA CHAN AS SERSI.

The film has a really diverse cast. What do you think that brings to the movie?
GC: I think it's exciting. I think it truly shows the scope of the film, and it's global. You see this great mix of people from lots of different backgrounds and cultures. And I just think it enriches the story that we're telling because it really is an epic, global story.

Would you say the Eternals have a family dynamic?
GC: Well, Ajak [played by Salma Hayek] is kind of our mother. She's the leader. Sprite [Lia McHugh] and Sersi are like sisters. They've been kind of thrown together a lot, and squabble a bit.

IKARIS AND SERSI,
AN ETERNAL LOVE STORY.

I would say each of the Eternals has a different bond with the others that is unique, and you see that as the film progresses. They have their own kind of bonds and rivalries. And there's playful rivalry, but also camaraderie between them. It's really fun. And having ten characters thrown together creates a really interesting mix. There were definitely some unexpected relationships and dynamics that came about that I would never have thought just from reading the script off the page.

What was it like to take this journey with Sersi?

GC: This is really a coming-of-age story for Sersi. She loves humans. She wants to fit in with them. So, she's been kind of operating under the radar. And her story in the film is really rediscovering her power, finding out that she needs to use that power to an even bigger extent than she ever thought.

And then, finding herself an unlikely leader of this group that she never thought she would lead. She's not the strongest, overtly. She's not the most powerful. She's not the loudest. So, she really becomes this unlikely hero as you go through the film. It's really nice to play a character who isn't the strongest when you meet her. She's a little bit uncertain, a little bit insecure, but by the end she really has come into her own, and come of age.

What was it like working with Kit Harington (Dane Whitman)?

GC: Kit Harington's lovely. He's great. And Dane and Sersi have a special bond, because he's really the first human that she's fallen in love with. And you can really understand why their relationship works. Dane is very assured, actually. There's a kind of quiet confidence about him that Sersi finds attractive. And, yeah, they have fun together as well. You can see why they'd be together, and why Sersi cares about him. It was really fun to play those scenes with Kit.

But what about Ikaris?

GC: Well, there is a love triangle of sorts. Sersi and Ikaris have a long history. I mean, they've been on and off for about 5,000 years! So, yeah, it's pretty long-term. I mean, what can I equate it to? I suppose Ikaris is that ex that you just can't shake. Is he good for you? Is he not good for you? I mean, she still has this attraction to him. And he to her.

But they've hurt each other in the past. For 5,000 years, they've been through everything together. And there's real love there, and a lot of history. But at the beginning of the film, Sersi has moved on. She's found someone else that she loves. And, of course, that's when Ikaris comes flying back into her life.

ABOVE: ANGELINA JOLIE AS THENA, LAUREN RIDLOFF AS MAKKARI, AND GEMMA CHAN AS SERSI.

Richard Madden speaks to us about Ikaris and his role within the Eternals team, what it was like working with Gemma Chan, and flying above London!

EVERLASTING LOYALTY

"I suppose one of the things I really enjoyed was being able to build this relationship with Ikaris and Sersi over the ages."

First question — what can you reveal about your character?
Richard Madden: I play Ikaris, one of the ten Eternals. At the beginning of the film, I think what's most important to Ikaris is the same thing that's most important to all Eternals, which is protecting intelligent life on earth.

Does that sort of attitude shift?
RM: Yes, as the movie goes on, Ikaris develops feelings for Sersi, one of the other Eternals, and that becomes his main focus, I suppose, after taking care of intelligent life on earth.

How are you alike or different from Ikaris?
RM: Well, very different. I can't fly. I can't shoot lasers out my eyes. I don't have super strength, all of the things I would very much like to have! Similarly, I suppose we both stick to our guns, and have a strong sense of duty and loyalty, I think. Those are some parallels we share, but it's quite hard to share parallels with someone who has been alive for thousands of years.

How did you bond with your fellow Eternals *actors?*
RM: In terms of bonding with some of my cast members, luckily, I'm very close with Gemma Chan [Sersi]. We've been friends for 10, 12 years. That's not quite the thousands of years that we need for these characters! But we've known each other for years before the film started, so that really helps in terms of building up a trust and a rapport with someone.

Speaking of Gemma Chan, what can you say about the relationship between Sersi and your character?
RM: I suppose one of the things I really enjoyed was being able to build this relationship with Ikaris and Sersi over the ages. I think it's a fascinating study of what keeps a couple together for thousands of years. Why do they not get bored each other? And what love means when you really care about someone for that length of time.

How would you describe Ikaris's relationship with the other Eternals?
RM: Ikaris is the right hand, I'd say, to Salma Hayek's character [Ajak]. He is the kind of loyal soldier, the right hand to the leader of the team.

Do you have any particular favorite moment from the film that you can share?
RM: One of my favorite moments to shoot, I suppose, was filming in Camden in London. I was on a crane on wires, and I'm flying and landing on the street. And that was really fun, just because I'm above the bridge in Camden, and I got a bird's-eye view of streets that I've walked for many years. So I got to see it from a different angle, and I really like that.

Eternals *is such a big movie with a large cast, yet it's full of smaller character moments. Can you talk to us a little about that?*
RM: I think what is really important about having ten characters is making sure that we get these little moments, these looks [between characters] after the scene is finished, or in between lines that are not purely there to move the plot forward or not there as scripted moments, but moments that we [as actors] managed to capture between two characters. These little moments elevate their characters and give them a bit of soul.

ABOVE: RICHARD MADDEN AS IKARIS USING HIS POWERS.

Salma Hayek talks about her role as the Eternals' guiding light, Ajak, developing her costume, and the first time she met her cast mates.

FOLLOW THE LEADER

"I really feel that I've created a special personal relationship with each one of the characters and each one of the actors..."

What would you say the stakes are in this film?
Salma Hayek: The stakes are always very high in the Marvel Studios movies — you know, you're often talking about the end of the world! And I think that in this particular film, because of the director [Chloé Zhao] and the way she shoots, her vision of it feels extra personal. This is amplified visually, and with the stakes. And it's a beautiful combination.

What can you tell us about your character, Ajak?
SH: Ajak is kind of the leader of the Eternals. She has to supervise all these amazingly powerful and intelligent beings that sometimes get bored and do crazy stuff, or sometimes get distracted and want to step away from the path of their mission. So, she has that job. She's also the only Eternal who can communicate with the Celestials.

And her power is healing. So, she has a very special relationship with each one of the Eternals. They're all different. And the way she approaches this leadership position is from a perspective a little like motherhood — which makes it different, I think, than most of the leaders in other movies. Ajak is very motherly. And at the end of the day, her choices are based on her motherly love for this amazing family.

What's your journey been like during the course of making this film?
SH: I really feel that I've created a special personal relationship with each one of the characters and each one of the actors, and made some really beautiful friendships. And I really feel like embracing them and keeping them together. I know it's part of my character, but it's really rubbed off on me!

How did you feel the first time you put on Ajak's costume?
SH: It's a little bit shocking when you see yourself in the costume for the first time, because you are trying to act with a lot of truth to the character and make her very human. Then, when you see yourself in the costume, you feel like it's Halloween or something! And there's a mixture of empowerment and also the joy of the child inside of me. It's fun. At the same time, I'm proud to wear this costume that means something important. I was lucky to work with Sammy Sheldon Differ, our costume designer, and put a lot of symbolic elements into it. They let me collaborate with them — we put a lot of work and a lot of love into Ajak's costume.

How would you describe your experience of working with the director, Chloé Zhao?
SH: I'm very happy to be part of this particular film for Marvel Studios because Chloé has a very specific vision for the movie. She uses our personalities and our diversity in a seamless way in the film, that's unifying at the same time as celebrating.

There is a family atmosphere on the set, and there's something very profound about the way Chloé approaches the characters and how she works with the actors. And I think the performances that I've seen are incredible. She really draws you into a character. And because we're playing these superhuman characters, I think it's really important to make sure we are able to feel all their emotions. They're Super Heroes, but somehow, the way she films it, makes it feel very intimate, and very real.

What's it been like working with your fellow cast members?
SH: I am really excited about the cast, not only because they are amazing actors, not only because of the talent, but because we are all so different. Yes, we are diverse. And this is extra exciting, to be able to be a part of a film by Marvel Studios that has the most diversity that we've ever seen in any Super Hero movie of all time. This moves me. It makes me feel part of something really special. There's something really beautiful about each one of these people that I am working with, beyond what I could've expected and what you can see. And we could not be more different from each other. And yet, we could not fit together more perfectly, on camera and off.

Do you remember meeting them for the first time?
SH: Well, coming together for the first time at [San Diego] Comic-Con was major, because there were so many people, and we had to present ourselves to everyone else at the same time that we were presenting ourselves to each other! And that was bizarre, and kind of scary.

SERSI AND IKARIS MARRY IN THE GUPTA EMPIRE.

Angelina Jolie talks about what separates her character, Thena, from the other Eternals, and the unique perspective of director Chloé Zhao.

A SOLDIER'S STORY

"Thena knows who she is in combat. But she doesn't know how to go to a party or socialize. She just doesn't have those skills."

What can you tell us about your character, Thena?
Angelina Jolie: Thena's a fighter. I think about her as somebody who, like a lot of soldiers, isn't comfortable in peacetime. They don't know how to exist as a civilian or as a lover or as a friend, but they know war. And she's kind of like that. Thena knows who she is in combat. But she doesn't know how to go to a party or socialize. She just doesn't have those skills.

What do you think makes Thena unique among her fellow Eternals?
AJ: You know, mental health is something that many people are talking about more than before, and it's such an important conversation. And Thena is somebody who is struggling with her mental health. In the movie, she doesn't kind of just "overcome it" and then be Thena. She is Thena, and has mental health issues. I think it's an important message. A lot of her struggles are ones that a lot of people will relate to for different reasons. Certainly soldiers — soldiers who are overwhelmed by the memories of all the battles and all they've seen. She just assumes that a fight's heading her way before she assumes that care and kindness are coming at her. So she's quite wired, and a lot of her struggle is just holding on to her mind and her center and her peace.

How would you describe Thena's relationship with Gilgamesh?
AJ: What's beautiful about [their relationship] is we are kind of soldiers in arms — two soldiers who have known each other and fought alongside each other. We're partners, real partners — even the way we fight, we fight together. We're that pairing of man and woman who are both physically and emotionally together. I feel like it's something different to see...to have a strong woman with a strong man, whom she leans on. It's the kind of male/female partnership that I'd like to see more of.

ABOVE: DON LEE AS GILGAMESH AND ANGELINA JOLE AS THENA, IN COSTUME.

What was it like when you first saw the costume, and the Eternals came together for the first time?

AJ: It was an interesting day! When you're alone and you're putting on that kind of an outfit, and you're standing there in your trailer and you're looking at yourself, you think, "What am I doing?" Because these costumes aren't the easiest things to put on! I think there'd be a really good behind-the-scenes of everybody trying to get their uniforms on. But what happened when we did all come together was, we were quite moved. And then, of course, we all laughed about who was gonna be who for Halloween. We were all gonna switch outfits. So I haven't figured out who I am yet. I'm working on it. I think Salma's gonna be Thena.

How do you develop a bond within the cast?

AJ: I don't know if this is the genius of [director] Chloé Zhao, but who she cast and how she cast us — it felt like we already knew each other. Very quickly, we were friends. I didn't have to work as hard, because my character isn't the most social. So if I was a little shy or awkward, or still not close to somebody, it was more Thena. But the person I had to be closest to [Gilgamesh], we naturally found each other immediately. Our characters were kind of inseparable, like me and [Gilgamesh actor] Don Lee.

You mentioned Chloé Zhao. What was it like working with her as the director?

AJ: She's an extraordinary choice. And I knew she'd bring something different. This is a huge movie. It is huge in scope and the span of time. It's huge in the effects and the new world creation. It's huge in that you have ten different, brand-new characters that you're introducing and creating — everything about them, their personalities, their backgrounds, their histories, their type of fighting. I don't know how she did it. I don't know how she was able to balance as much. But what I wasn't surprised by was the authenticity Chloé brought to the movie. It's kind of the most epic sort of supernatural film, yet it feels very, very personal and very emotional and very human. I'm not sure how she did it, but I believe that's her gift.

Last question — do you have a favorite moment or scene from the film?

AJ: You know what's really fun for me? I was so excited seeing everybody else's great scene. It's because I know these actors. I know their characters. I see the family being built. It is so rare that you see a film and there is this equality of contribution and expression within the piece by everyone. And so when I'm watching, I'd think, "Oh, he nailed that!" Or, "That was so beautiful!" Or, "Oh, she did that. I loved that speech!" I was kind of in awe of everybody else in the film.

THENA IN A MOMENT OF PEACE
IN THE WOODS.

Gilgamesh actor Don Lee talks about playing the Eternals' strongman, being part of a team, and joining the Marvel Cinematic Universe.

STRONG WORDS

"Gilgamesh is like the big, older brother. We are like one family... sometimes we take care of each other. Sometimes we fight each other."

So what was it like, joining the Marvel Cinematic Universe?
Don Lee: I've always been a big fan of the Marvel Cinematic Universe. The films and the Marvel comics both, actually. And I played many real-life hero characters in many Korean movies before. But I really wanted to become a Marvel Super Hero. That dream came true, and I was so excited. I'm so honored to be a part of the ten [Eternals].

What was it like, working with this group of actors?
DL: It was amazing. Seeing all those talented people from all over the world. And then we felt like the Eternals already. That was great. I think everyone found their roles pretty quickly — not just in the film, but in real life, too. So, we have come to feel like family together. We got close so easily. And that really helped our acting, too.

What can you tell us about your character, Gilgamesh?
DL: He's one of the strongest and most powerful characters in the Eternals. His specialty is super strength and a super punch. And also, he's a fun-loving, entertaining character, so hopefully people will love him. He's a well-rounded character, so I love playing Gilgamesh.

How would you describe Gilgamesh's relationship with the other Eternals?
DL: Gilgamesh is like the big, older brother. We are like one family. So, just like family members, sometimes we take care of each other. Sometimes we fight each other. And then, especially with Thena [played by Angelina Jolie], Gilgamesh always tries to take care of her. He loves her like a big brother or a father. He's a protector for Thena.

What was it like seeing yourself in costume for the first time?
DL: Okay, so I felt like I became a real Super Hero right after I wore that! I love the costume.

Have you had a favorite moment from the filming?
DL: There's a scene where I'm dropping pie. We had to do it around ten times, because of the different camera angles. And then we kind of couldn't stop laughing. So, we really had a hard time shooting it! But it was really, really fun.

How was it working with the director, Chloé Zhao?
DL: Not just for this movie, but I think Chloé's the best choice for a lot of different movies. The heroes of the Eternals have a deep sense of conflict with their identities. You can see in her previous movies that Chloé gives a life to the character. And she's an incredible director. The best thing she always does is making the characters come alive. That's the perfect skill for this movie.

ABOVE: GILGAMESH AND THENA SHARE A DEEP FRIENDSHIP.

We spoke to Sprite actress Lia McHugh, who told us what it was like to be the youngest member of the Eternals.

ETERNAL TRICKSTER

"Sprite's like the cranky old lady and the trickster. She kind of just tells it to you flat-out how it is."

What was it that made you want to join the Marvel Cinematic Universe?

Lia McHugh: Everything about the movies made me want to join! I love that they're action and adventure, but also comedy and also drama. I like how each of them are different. Like, the *Guardians of the Galaxy* movies are really funny. And the *Iron Man* movies are really sad, but also have funny moments, and they're action-packed. I love all the characters and how they've been developed. It's really cool.

How did it feel, stepping into this ensemble of very talented actors?

LM: I think we all just clicked immediately. And every day on set, we all just become more of a family. And everyone's always helping each other out, you know, forgetting a line, giving them a script, giving each other tips. I have the best time on set. It's really fun to learn about all these different people and about their lives and experiences in acting, especially for me, 'cause I'm just a kid.

Who are the Eternals?

LM: This film is about the Eternals coming and blending into society and helping humans to grow. They're protecting the humans by fighting the Deviants, while they're sort of helping people nurture their culture.

What can you tell us about your character, Sprite?

LM: Sprite can create illusions. And she can make herself and other people invisible, which I think is really cool. I guess you could say she's fiery, with a little bit of a temper. She's really sarcastic and annoyed, I would say, most of the time. Sprite's kinda like the old soul in the group, the grumpy one.

What's it like for Sprite being one of the oldest Eternals?

LM: It's really weird to be old, but physically be in the body of a child. It was a weird thing to figure out. Chloé is an amazing director. And we had a lot of conversations. She really took me through it and helped me to understand more about how Sprite was feeling.

How would you describe your journey with the character?

LM: Every day is different on set, and every day I get to know her better. We started filming slow, in individual scenes, and [the actors] got to know each other better. It helps you to establish the relationships for when you do big scenes with all the ten of the Eternals. Now, the big scenes are so easy because we all have our established relationships. I love my relationship with Kingo [Kumail Nanjiani]. It's really funny. And we're actually like that in real life. We mess with each other a lot. We were all just this big family.

What kind of role do you think Sprite plays in the Eternals family?

LM: Sprite's like the cranky old lady and the trickster. She kind of just tells it to you flat-out how it is. She doesn't sugarcoat anything. I think she's a really funny character overall.

You mentioned director Chloé Zhao earlier. What was it like working with her?

LM: Chloé's involved in every single aspect of the film, and she's really looking at it all in the big picture and putting it all together to make this amazing film. She's invested in each individual character. She's really cool, and so fun to hang out with on set, too. She's doing like a hundred things at once! I don't know how she does it, but it's amazing.

Chloé's so perceptive in every single little moment of the film. And she's always thinking of what she can do better. And she's never stuck in a point of view. She just wants to make it the best that it can be. And it's so fun to talk to her about it and to figure it out together. And I absolutely love her. She's so sweet.

It seems like one of the themes of this movie is being stronger together.

LM: It's a beautiful message. When we all come together, we're stronger, and we're not as strong when we're fighting against each other, or on our own. And in the movie, we all separate at a certain point, and then we come back together. That's when we can actually make an impact because we're all together and really connecting.

LIA MCHUGH FILMS
A SCENE AS SPRITE.

Phastos actor Brian Tyree Henry talks about his intellectual character, how he got the part, and the joys of working on set.

MAN OF SCIENCE

"I really wanted to find Phastos on my own. There was no one way to play him. No one has played him before. So, I really wanted to embody him on my own."

How did you come to be a part of Eternals*?*
Brian Tyree Henry: You know, it's very interesting, because I never in a million years thought I'd be a part of the Marvel Cinematic Universe. It's an interesting story, 'cause I was filming a movie in Australia recently, and I went to go see *Captain Marvel*. And I was like, "Yeah, Captain Marvel!" You know, I was really into it. And when the credits came on I was like, "Oh, well, okay, that's it, guys. I'm not gonna be a part of the Marvel Cinematic Universe." And my friends were like, "Why would you say that?" I was like, "Well, you know, I just don't feel like there's anybody that looks like me, that is like me up there [on the screen]." And literally two days later, I kid you not, I got a call from Chloé Zhao requesting that I be a part of *Marvel Studios' Eternals*. So, it was great. But, yeah, man, I have always been a huge fan.

I've been obsessed with the concept of Super Heroes and that kind of concept of mankind needing saving. And I think that when you get this group of people together who just have these innate senses of superpowers and saving humanity, it's something that we all kinda need. And it literally brings everyone together regardless of where you're from. You could be in Africa. You could be in Antarctica and you could still be like, "Oh, yeah, Iron Man is everything. And the Hulk is everything." And it's just something about that kind of hope, honestly, that the Marvel Cinematic Universe does. I'm still freaking out that I'm a part of it. I come on set, and I'm just like, "Oh, right, okay, we're doing it. I'm a Super Hero!"

How did you prepare for your role as Phastos?
BTH: I really wanted to find Phastos on my own. There was no one way to play him. No one has played him before. So, I really wanted to embody him on my own. And what's really great about the casting of this movie is that Chloé is so remarkable, because we really are kinda playing ourselves. We really embody ourselves. We embody all our weaknesses, all our strong parts. It really is just us stepping up to the plate as ourselves. And for Phastos, especially, he is the engineer of the group. He is, I don't want to say the smart one, but he is! He is also the glue to the Eternals, because he is the one that can basically maneuver both sides with the fighters and the intellectuals.

What else can you tell us about your character?
BTH: So, the Eternals are all based off pure energy, given to us by the Celestials — like the purest form of energy that's in the universe. That's just within us. It allows us to restore ourselves. It keeps us immortal. We don't age. [And the Eternals are] split in two groups. There are five fighters, and there are five intellectuals. And I'm one of the intellectuals. That doesn't mean I don't fight. Let's just get that clear.

ABOVE: BRIAN TYREE HENRY AS PHASTOS IN CIVILIAN CLOTHES.

Phastos is the scientist. Everything he does, he does for the advancement of humankind. So, he's created different things like steam engines. He probably even taught people how to make the wheel. They like to call me the technopath, which basically means I can use my mind and my energy to literally assemble anything out of any technology around me. And can I talk to machines? Maybe. But you can't really do that in public without people thinking you're crazy.

He's also one of the kindest characters I've ever met, which is really nice, because I have a reputation of playing really tough characters. I have a reputation of being really hard. And what I like about Phastos is that he is really just love. There's something about humanity that he sees, regardless of the downfalls that we've gone through. He still has hope.

How would you describe the stakes in the film?
BTH: The stakes are, if we don't save humanity and defeat the Deviants, then everything will be destroyed. You may have thought [the same thing] like in the *Avengers* movies when you had all of the Thanos stuff. No. This is literally like it's over. It's really over.

What's it been like working with Chloé Zhao?
BTH: Because she is like the one that will come in and just be as messy as possible, she gets the messiest things out of us. There's nothing greater than watching your director see you do something and get excited where she jumps from behind the camera and runs up. She makes you want to try stuff. She makes you want to believe in her vision — and the vision includes you and how you craft it and how you mold it. So, there's a lot of improv.

LEFT: BRIAN TYREE HENRY AS PHASTOS, WHILE CREATING PROTOTYPES IN HIS STUDIO.

Makkari herself, Lauren Ridloff, told us what it was like playing the fastest member of the Eternals, as well as Marvel Studios' first deaf Super Hero.

THE AMAZING MAKKARI

"Makkari is probably the sister within the group. She's smart, and very levelheaded. And at the same time, she's the wild card."

What's been your experience with the Marvel Cinematic Universe?

Lauren Ridloff: Wow, that is a loaded question! I've always known about the Marvel Cinematic Universe. My first impression of it probably was *Iron Man* (2008). That's probably my first look into the Marvel Cinematic Universe. And I've never once dreamt that I would be a part of that universe. It's still so amazing to me, being on set and just working with the amazing team that's behind everything that happens. I'm just in deep awe about the dedication that I see behind the Marvel Cinematic Universe.

What kind of research did you do for your role?

LR: I did a lot of research into mythology, working with the American Sign Language consultant. It actually helps us with the translation process, and also developing name signs for each character within the movie.

As an actor, what's it been like working with director Chloé Zhao?

LR: I have to give a hats off to Chloé, 'cause I think she really allows those character relationships to develop organically over time. And understand, at the very beginning, we had our first meeting with Chloé. We talked about the general idea of what our relationships would be with specific characters. And while we took on those ideas, they have completely evolved as our bonding deepens.

Why do you think Chloé is the perfect choice to direct this film?

LR: Well, first of all, Chloé has the eye. When you see her work on the big screen, it is amazing. And I think what really exemplifies her work thus far, they all represent her value of the Earth. You see how much she actually loves this place, this planet we call home, and she reflects that in the film. And at the same time, Chloé has this ability to really hone in on one character. Somehow, she makes each of the ten Eternals become the center character.

In the film, you play Makkari. What can you tell us about her?

LR: I love Makkari. Obviously, she's fast. That's her power, but also, she's loyal. And she values her family. She would do anything for her family. She would do what's right. But also, Makkari's not a Goody Two-Shoes. She's not a saint. She does steal quite a bit. She likes shiny objects. And I mean, come on, she's been on this planet for 7,000 years! So, Makkari picks up a few things that she likes.

What's at stake for Makkari and her fellow Eternals?

LR: Well, humanity. I have to say, I feel like the stakes in this story are epic.

How would you describe Makkari's relationship with the other Eternals?

LR: We're a dysfunctional family. And so, I think Makkari has a specific relationship with specific Eternals. And Makkari is probably the sister within the group. She's smart, and very levelheaded. And at the same time, she's the wild card. So, the whole family kind of looks to Makkari for the final answer.

How does it feel, playing Marvel Studios' first deaf Super Hero?

LR: Honestly, I'm just so excited to think about having deaf kids wearing Halloween costumes that are going to be Makkari inspired! I think that is the most important thing about having a deaf Super Hero on the big screen. It shows that there's so much more to every individual, regardless of their ability. And I'm just so happy to see that there's a deaf character that is contributing to a story within the Marvel Cinematic Universe.

If there's one word that embodies Makkari, what would it be?

LR: Speedster. Yeah, speedster.

You described the Eternals as a dysfunctional family, yet they come together.

LR: Yes, I do think that's very important. I think what's so great, and what I love about the Eternals, is that they do have the specific strengths on their own. Which is very good, but it's not quite enough until they all come together. Each Eternal complements the other, and you can see that even in the color of their Super Hero costumes.

Actor Barry Keoghan talks about playing Druig, his love of Super Heroes, and his favorite moment in *Eternals*.

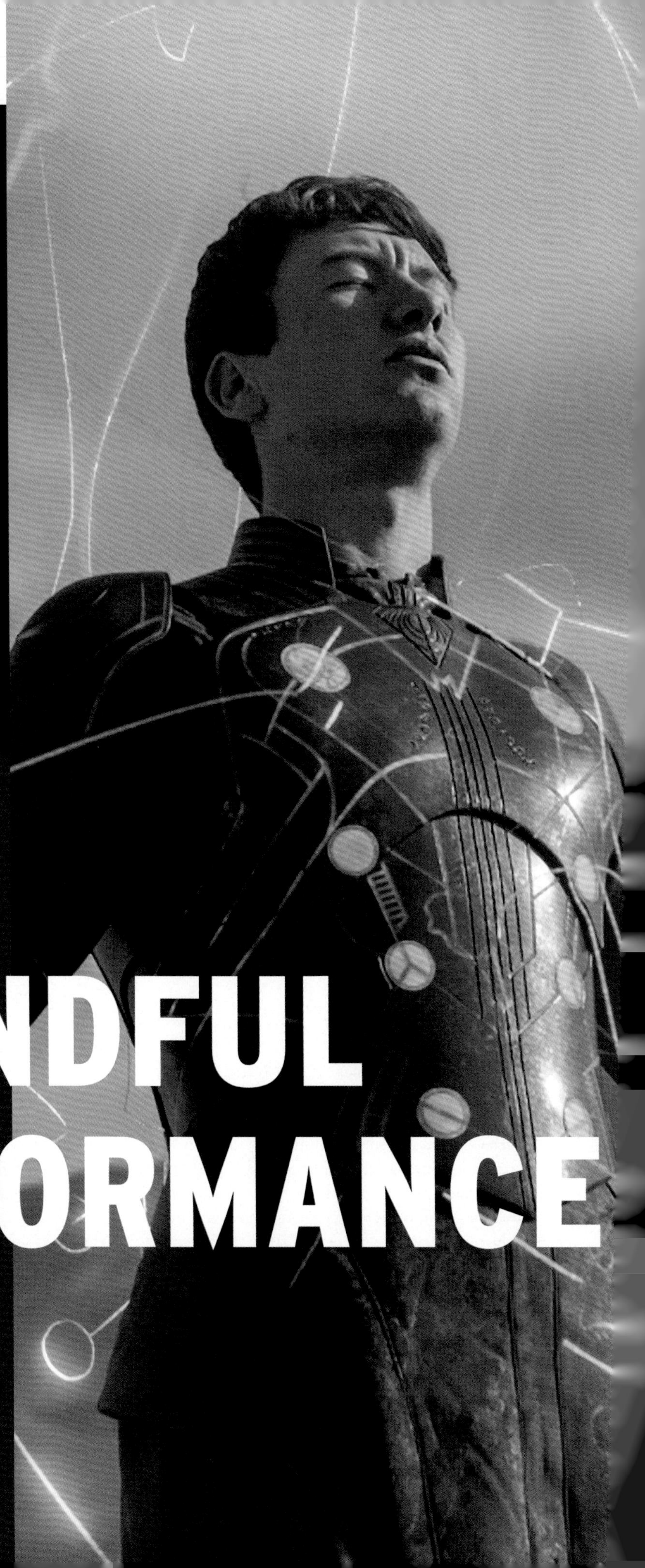

A MINDFUL PERFORMANCE

"...when I heard Chloé Zhao was doing a Marvel Studios movie I was like, 'Oh, I'd love to be a part of that and see how she gets in behind this Super Hero world and makes it her own.'"

How excited were you to become a part of this movie?
Barry Keoghan: I mean, it's always a kid's dream to be a Super Hero. When I was told I was gonna be part of it, I was pumped! I'm a big comic book fan. And I love collectibles and stuff like that. Even in school, when I was younger, I used to create characters and give them powers. So, I think it was just an element of that, wanting to be a part of that world.

What can you tell us about your character, Druig?
BK: He's obviously the coolest one out of all of them and the best one, not only 'cause I'm playing him. [laughs] That actually adds another factor to it, but, no, Druig's power is mind control. He's just very well composed, and can put everyone in sync and make them do whatever he wants. That's his power, kind of like manipulation.

What was it like first seeing the costume?
BK: I always say, as soon as you put the boots on, your posture changes. You definitely change your whole demeanor, and everything changes.

What would've eight-year-old Barry thought of you in costume?
BK: Yeah, yeah, I don't know. I'm still processing! I don't think it's hit me yet that I'm doing a Marvel Studios movie! And I think that's how Chloé Zhao shoots it and how she directs it. Even though it's a Super Hero world, she somehow makes it very, very real. So, I haven't got that whole Super Hero feeling yet. I don't know how eight-year-old Barry would think.

You mentioned director Chloé Zhao. What's it been like working with her?
BK: For me, her previous movie, *The Rider*, was so raw and real and almost like a documentary, kind of. It let you in, in a way that not a lot of movies let you in. And when I heard Chloé Zhao was doing a Marvel Studios movie I was like, "Oh, I'd love to be a part of that and see how she gets in behind this Super Hero world and makes it her own." When I heard she was on board I was even more keen to sign up.

She's very easy to work with. She'll mention a few words to me, and I'll switch it up for her. And she knows how to get what she wants but in the fewest words. So, we have a great relationship like that.

Do you have a favorite moment from the film?
BK: Walking down the steps of the Aztec, which was very tricky because the steps were very, very steep. And I had to look at the camera when I'm walking down, and just hope that I get to the next step and play it cool.

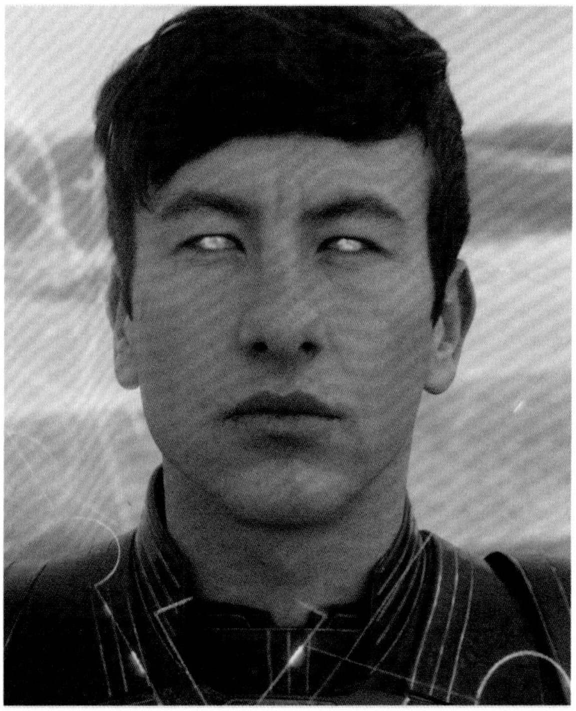

ABOVE: DRUIG WHILE MIND CONTROLLING.

Kumail Nanjiani discusses his character, and learning how to dance Bollywood style.

DANCE FIGHT

"...if you'd asked me five years ago, 'What's your big dream?', I would've said, 'I'd love to be in the Marvel Cinematic Universe.'"

What made you want to become a part of the Marvel Cinematic Universe?

Kumail Nanjiani: I've been a fan of these characters my whole life. I've been a big comic book fan, and I always look forward to these movies. When the Marvel Cinematic Universe started, I remember watching *Iron Man* and just being blown away by it. It seemed to really capture so many different things about these comic books. It was obviously thrilling, and the action was great.

But it was also really funny, and it had this deftness and lightness to it. I really like that. Then, as the Marvel Cinematic Universe developed, I was really impressed by how all the movies linked up with each other, made each other better, but also stood on their own. And I just became a huge fan of these movies. I can't think of a series of movies that have all been this good, ever, in history.

And, honestly, if you'd asked me five years ago, "What's your big dream?", I would've said, "I'd love to be in the Marvel Cinematic Universe." So, for me it wasn't a decision to join. It was their decision to ask me, and when they did, I said, yes!

Did you do any particular kind of research before you started work on the movie?

KN: I read the original Jack Kirby *The Eternals* comics. And for me, particularly for my character, I went back and watched a lot of Bollywood movies again to prepare for this role. I grew up watching Bollywood movies. And this guy, Kingo, is a Bollywood movie star. So, I know that world really well.

Can you introduce us to your character, Kingo?

KN: Kingo is one of the fighters of the group. [The Eternals have] basically split up from each other a long time ago, and we're all supposed to keep a low profile. So, Kingo decided to keep a low profile by becoming a Bollywood movie star. That's where he is at the beginning of the movie. He's this guy who's always been pretty flashy. He's sort of always wanted people to know he's a Super Hero, but he can't reveal that. To him, this is the second best thing. People won't know he's a Super Hero, but everyone's gonna know he's a movie star. He's just really flashy, really enjoys his life, really enjoys his fame, really enjoys his money, and really, really loves his family. He really misses the Eternals. So, when he's called back to the mission in the beginning, [there's some regret], you know, a little bit of, "Oh, so, I have to leave my movie star life behind." But he gets to fight with his family, so he's very excited about that.

Oh, yeah, and he can shoot energy from his hands, and he's very flamboyant in the way he fights.

What's the scope of the film like?

KN: I really think this is the most epic movie that Marvel Studios has done, and I don't mean "epic" in sort of the new Internet sense. I mean "epic" in the traditional sense. This movie spans thousands of years. We start off 7,000 years ago, and we come all the way to the present. It spans multiple time periods.

Can you describe what it's been like, working with director Chloé Zhao?

KN: I've been a huge fan of hers before this. So, when I heard she was directing this movie — this was before I was on board, obviously — I was very excited, 'cause the Marvel Cinematic Universe has been so good at taking very idiosyncratic directors that have made very idiosyncratic movies and then having them bring their vision to a big scale. I was very excited to see Chloé's version of it.

I didn't quite understand what [that vision] would be. When I met her, immediately, it made sense. Her movies don't shy away from dark emotions. But she's not like that. She's very sunny. She's very, very smart, but she also likes to have this childish enthusiasm. And she's a huge fan of the Marvel Cinematic Universe and comic books. She's like a hardcore

RIGHT: KUMAIL NANJIANI AS KINGO IN CENTER OF BOLLYWOOD DANCE NUMBER.

nerd. She knows everything there is to know about Marvel. And obviously, she brings a lot of gravitas to the movie, 'cause that's the work that she's done before. And she brings a lot of character work and specific relationship moments. But her vision about the scale of it is also so clear. And that's been the part that to me has been the most surprising. I knew she'd get the character stuff. I knew she'd get the relationship stuff. But her stuff with the action, she has just a specific way she wants things to look, and it's great. It's really, really good. I don't like to watch myself. But every now and then, there'll be an action scene we shoot, and she's like, "Do you want to come see it?" So I'll look, and it's like no other action scene I've seen in a Marvel Studios movie or otherwise.

Do you have a favorite moment or scene?
KN: It's the one I've worked on the most — my character's introduction in the present is on a Bollywood movie set. And he does this big Bollywood dance number. I would say I'm most excited just to watch that scene, 'cause I don't dance. I don't know how to dance. Do you know we'd started shooting it, and Chloé was like, "Hey, just so you know, I'm writing you a big dance sequence." And I was like, "I'm full of fear. That sounds amazing. Get me a dance teacher right now."

And I worked with [a dance teacher] for months before we actually shot that scene. We were choreographing and working on it. And it just was so much fun to do, and there were like 50 backup dancers. And it's this massive Bollywood set. So, I gotta say, that's the one I'm most excited to see. I hope all the work paid off. It looks beautiful.

Last question. If you had to describe Kingo in one word, what would it be?
KN: Joy. I think he's really full of joy. I think he really is excited about everything all the time.

KINGO LIVES THE LIFE AS A BOLLYWOOD SUPERSTAR.

Kit Harington, who portrays Dane Whitman, talks about humanity, love triangles, and working with director Chloé Zhao.

WHITMAN'S WORDS

"Dane is the human element of the story. He represents humanity... and I think he really represents all those things that Sersi loves about the planet."

What are your impressions of the Marvel Cinematic Universe, and what made you excited to join it?
Kit Harington: Marvel Studios has been a huge part of cinema, a huge part of the cinematic experience. I've had friends who've done Marvel movies. I've always kind of been rather jealous of them! So, to come round to a place where I'm being involved in this universe, it's huge, a great gift. It's a fantastic thing. I'm thrilled. It's one of those calls that you want to get as an actor. Like, "Right, they want you to come into the Marvel Cinematic Universe and to be part of their storytelling!"

What can you tell us about your character, Dane Whitman?
KH: Whilst not being an Eternal, Dane is the human element of the story. He represents humanity. Sersi is an Eternal. She's been around forever, obviously, as the name suggests, but is a recent partner of Dane. And I think he really represents all those things that Sersi loves about the planet. He's meant to kind of stand in for Earth and humanity. So, within that, we get his kind of quite dry sense of humor, his affection, the way he speaks, the way he moves and talks.

We understand there's something of a love triangle...
KH: Yeah, Dane and Sersi are part of a love triangle, which includes Ikaris. Yeah, poor old Dane, he's up against quite the competition with Ikaris. I mean, not only is he [played by] Richard Madden, but it's a guy who shoots lasers out of his eyes and flies. Dane is a museum scientist. So, I felt Dane had to have a quiet confidence about himself that meant he could stand toe-to-toe with a giant such as that, and not be afraid. I think Dane's one of those guys who's from a certain schooling background where they've taught him not to be afraid of anyone. And what Sersi loves about him is this self-assuredness. He can stand opposite Ikaris who's just destroyed a monster and say, "Hi, I'm Dane!" and hopefully not come off too badly, but we'll see. Sersi's stuck between two men, who represent entirely different things. I'm pretty happy about what I represent in the film, but hopefully it'll be an interesting story line for the audience to watch.

What can you tell us about the size and scope of the film?
KH: I love that this was shot on location. I didn't expect that. When I signed up for this movie I thought, "Oh, I'll be in a big green box in a studio somewhere." And I was wrong. I think I've been in the studio one day out of all my days I've been here. I realized the scope of a production like this when I was filming all round near my house. I live in north London. And this is ideal for me, this movie filming all near me.

But it was the night shoots where they shut down Camden that I kind of went, "Wow, this is – they can do this? They can shut down one of the busiest parts of London for us to film here?" That's a lot of ambition. I was sad the day I was in the studio. I like being out on set. I like being outside.

What does director Chloé Zhao bring to the production?
KH: I think Chloé Zhao's the reason why this film was shot so much on location. She wanted to do a Marvel movie that was steeped in real places, real locations. And that's her film work. That's the kind of way she shoots. And I think that's gonna be really interesting. I think that's gonna mark this film out from other Marvel Studios movies.

What are you most excited for audiences to experience?
KH: I think that Marvel Studios is moving into new territory. This is a new world, a new set of characters. I think that's the thing that's incredible about the Marvel Cinematic Universe. It just has this host of fascinating, flawed characters running alongside each other. It's an incredibly complex universe. And I think that [this film] takes it that next step. I'm really excited to be part of it.

KIT HARINGTON AND GEMMA CHAN
SHOOT A SCENE IN LONDON.

Actor Harish Patel talks about what it's like to be a human amongst the Eternals.

THE HUMAN TOUCH

"The comedy in the movie is because there is only one human being amongst all these powerful Super Heroes..."

How did you become involved in this movie?
Harish Patel: [The casting process] had taken two months. I had sent my [audition] tape, but there was no reply, nothing. And I was asking my agent, "Well, what is there?" So, she told me, "Oh, don't worry. You are in the mix." And then I got a call that they wanted to screen-test me.

What can you tell us about your character, Karun?
HP: Well, he is actually Kingo's valet, but he's also his friend, philosopher, and kind of guide. And he treats him like his son.

The character adds a bit of comedy to the film.
HP: The comedy in the movie is because there is only one human being amongst all these powerful Super Heroes, extra-strong kind of people. So, naturally, he watches their fights and their powers, and the comedy [comes from that].

Have you had a favorite scene that you worked on?
HP: Well, all the scenes are my favorite. All the scenes are funny! All the scenes are very good. The scene [we shot today] was so funny.

What's it been like working with director Chloé Zhao?
HP: She is like one of us. Yeah, she also acts. She takes opinions. She also talks about the scenes. She will keep improvising. And she listens to you. This is what's good about her.

What journey do you hope audiences go on?
HP: They'll feel like a child, even though they are of my age, you know? I'm a senior citizen, but they'll feel like a child. They'll enjoy [the movie] like a child. Because I feel the same way watching these films.

ABOVE: KUMAIL NANJIANI AS KINGO AND HARISH PATEL AS KARUN.

Take a look at the concept art that powered the creation of *Eternals*.

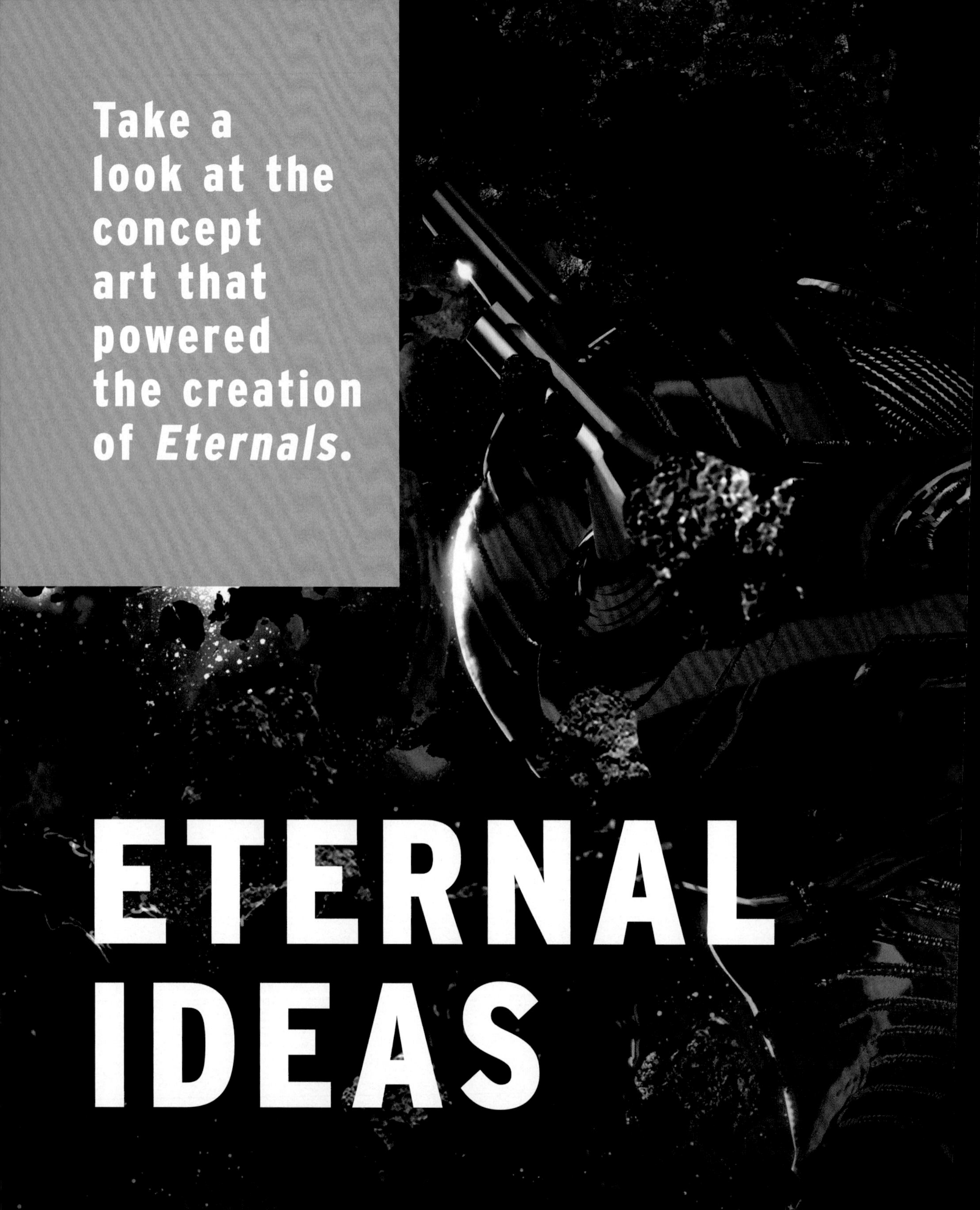

ETERNAL IDEAS

A GLIMPSE AT ONE OF THE CELESTIALS.
ART BY RODNEY FUENTEBELLA.

ABOVE: A BATTLE IS BREWING IN AN AZTEC CITY.
ART BY ALEXANDER MANDRADJIEV.

ABOVE: SERSI TRANSMUTES A BUS INTO FLOWERS.
ART BY ALEXANDER MANDRADJIEV.

ABOVE: THE ETERNALS ATTEND FESTIVITIES IN ANCIENT BABYLON.
ART BY JACKSON SZE.

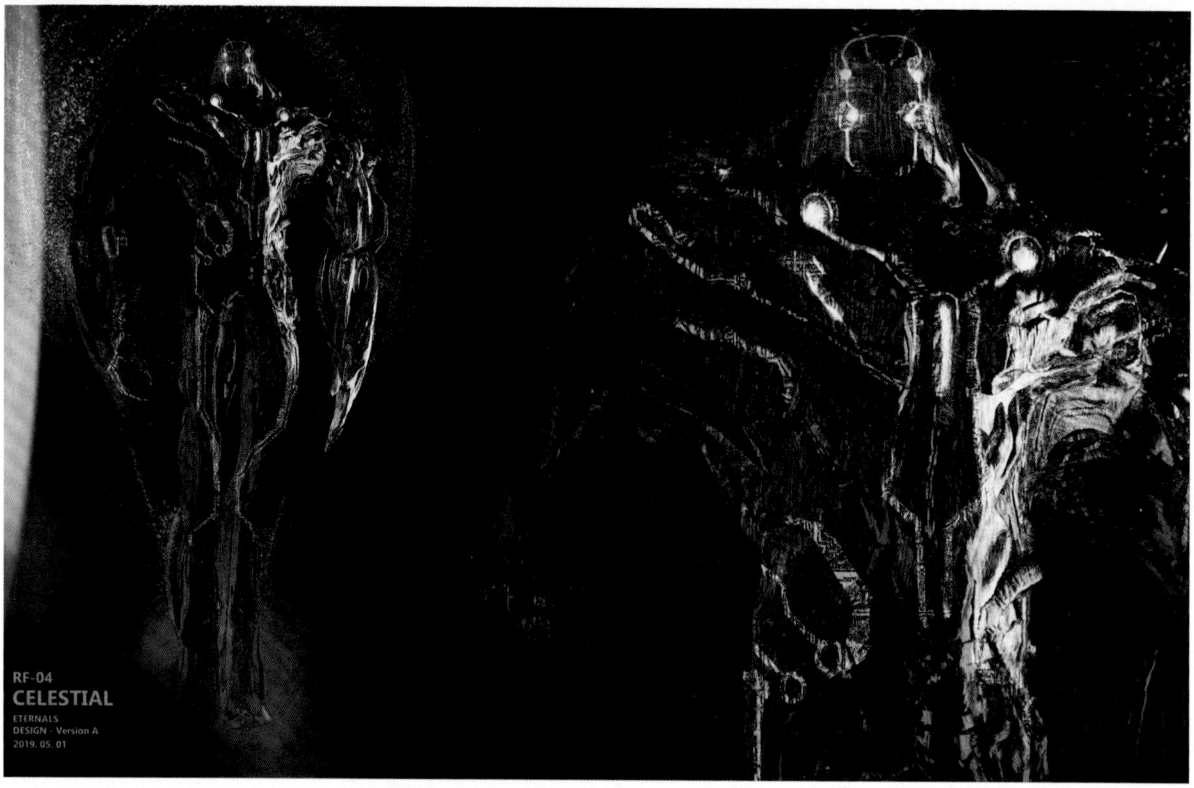

ABOVE: A STUDY OF A CELESTIAL.
ART BY RODNEY FUENTEBELLA.

ABOVE: THE HANGING GARDENS OF BABYLON.
ART BY ALEXANDER MANDRADJIEV.

ABOVE: A STUDY OF ARISHEM, THE CELESTIAL.
ART BY RODNEY FUENTEBELLA.

Take an inside look at the Eternals' costumes by Ivo Coveney and Sammy Sheldon Differ.

GETTING THE LOOK

"It was more about making sure the costumes all worked in the same universe, even though each costume is very different." – Ivo Coveney

What is your favorite part of designing costumes for Marvel Studios?
Sammy Sheldon Differ (Costume Designer): It's always a challenge, first of all. When I first read this script, I thought, "Wow, this has got everything!" It's got all different [time] periods. It's got future, past, you know, everything. So, from a costume design perspective, there's a lot there to play with. It's super exciting. And on top of that, you know you're gonna design ten new Super Heroes. So when they said, "Do you want to do it?", I was like, "Yeah!"

Can you tell us a little about the process for the costume design?
SSD: You look at each character, and you start analyzing them as a person, and put colors and textures and feelings to them, and try and personify them. We did a lot of research into the galaxy, the cosmos, and light and energy — all those elements, the earth and planets, and just tried to get a framework of colors and textures that we could pull on, particularly when it came to designing the Super Hero looks. Because what was needed, and what was asked for, was something that wasn't like a Super Hero suit as such, but more like a second skin. Conceptually, it was a difficult thing to get your head around because there were areas on the bodies that were carved into and then areas that came out. We were trying to deal with elements that can't be made like clothes and can't be made like armor. We experimented with tons of different stretch [materials], non-stretch, shiny, matte, gold, with the layers over, everything. We experimented for months and months, and eventually came to a plan. And once we had that plan with the color and the texture, then we brought back in all the historical research that we could then implement throughout their journeys we see in the film.

Before we turn it over to Ivo Coveney, do you have a favorite moment from the time spent working on the film?
SSD: I think... gosh, I mean, I love all ten costumes! I really do. I really love their Super Hero costumes. And when we started [the process], we spent about four or five months experimenting before we could actually get anything vaguely cut out and molded. And I honestly wasn't sure that we'd get there. I really wasn't! I'm so proud of what my team has done, because they really are amazing. The textures are there. The finish on them is brilliant. And to top it all off, I really thought we'd have a lot of damage from all the stunts and everything. And the costumes have stayed together. So, it's quite amazing.

What's your specific role on this film?
Ivo Coveney (Head Specialty Costume Creator): Sammy Sheldon Differ and I have known one another for over 30 years. We met at the Manchester Royal Exchange when both in our teens. We've worked

ABOVE: MAKKARI ARMOR DETAILS ILLUMINATING AS SHE RECEIVES HER POWERS AGAIN.

ABOVE: FIVE OF THE ETERNALS IN THEIR ARMOR.

together a lot as we've gone through our careers, at various stages. And since she's become a designer, I've worked with her for the last 10, 15 years on most of her films. We have a very good working relationship.

For me, the joy of that is she trusts me. So, if she comes up with something, or when she gets a concept, she allows me to play with that concept so I feel that I'm involved. Sammy knows what she wants. She'll say to me, "Here's a concept," but I feel that myself and my team are involved in the process. That's far more rewarding for me.

What were some of the inspirations for the Eternals' costumes?

IC: It starts with [Head of Visual Development] Ryan Meinerding working with the director over in L.A. for a while. And then Sammy Sheldon Differ, my costume designer, gets involved with Ryan, and they start working out the concepts. So, by the time I see them, the concepts are fairly well realized.

My job is then to get those concepts, and figure out how to make those fit real bodies, fit the actors. So, the minute I see the designs, I am working out how the costumes would actually move. And then it's conversations with Sammy and with [Director] Chloé Zhao about how they want those to be realized in 3-D.

Can you talk about the intent behind the costumes?

IC: Chloé's very keen on the Jack Kirby illustrations from the comics. And we made sure that a lot of circles with lines through them featured in all of the detailing of all of our pieces [to reflect that look]. It was more about making sure the costumes all worked in the same universe, even though each costume is very different.

What's the biggest challenge you've faced working on this film?

IC: There was a big struggle trying to make sure that the fabric was right. I know Sammy worked very hard with Chloé to make sure that the fabrics worked. We were taking our lead from the fabric. So, we didn't know how we were gonna be painting our pieces until the fabrics were locked down. And then all of our pieces are incredibly labor-intensive for paintwork. We had to work out how we could get things done. When we finally knew who all of our actors were and filming began, we had to really plan how we were gonna get things made, cast, molded, and painted. And there were times that we just didn't think we would.

Do you have a favorite moment from making the film?

IC: Brian Tyree Henry's final fitting. It was just absolutely my favorite moment on this film. In any fitting I've ever done, actors are often happy with [our work], and they're thankful. But Brian was so excited. And then, when he did turn around [and see himself in the mirror], he just screamed. "Scream" is not the right word. He yelled, and he just said, "Oh, my god, this is amazing!" And what was brilliant is, everyone else in the costume room could hear him. I went outside, and I saw people looking over 'cause they were worried something was wrong! And he was so happy, and then he actually burst into tears. He just said, "I never thought I would be a Super Hero." And that's just amazing. And then he asked for the women that had made his costume to come into the room. They came in, and he thanked them. He's just such a gentleman and such a lovely man. That's my favorite moment that I'll take away from this film.

ABOVE: PHASTOS IN COSTUME.
BELOW: ETERNALS IN CIVILIAN CLOTHES WHILE EXPLORING THE DESERT.

Costume Designer Sammy Sheldon Differ takes a look at the movie's costumes, Eternal by Eternal.

CLOTHES MADE ETERNAL

IKARIS

Sammy Sheldon Differ: Ikaris is strong. He's arrogant. He wants to control everything. He wants to be in charge. And he doesn't deviate from anything, so he's true to what he believes. So, his look, his Super Hero costume, looks very muscular. And it's very tapered in at the waist. And it has this slightly gladiatorial feel about the skirted part of it. As we go through time with him, everything is quite fitted and very straight and tailored. There's nothing complicated about his clothing.

SERSI

SSD: Sersi loves humanity. She's a very giving person. And the color that we gave her was basically green and silver. She's soft as well. It's not super structured. It's a bit more ethereal, really. And then as she comes into the modern world, [her look is] quite funky. She likes nice jumpers, and she likes to wear bits and pieces. It's easy clothing, really.

ABOVE: SERSI AND IKARIS IN THEIR CASUAL LOOK.

MAKKARI
THENA
AJAK

THE ETERNALS' WARDROBE.

AJAK

SSD: Ajak loves nature. She loves animals, anything to do with nature on Earth. And she is also the leader, and has the link to the Celestials. So, she's very much got this kind of goddess feel about her. As we go through time, she keeps that nobility through her looks. Until we get to the modern world, where she's very much with the Earth. She likes jeans and easy clothing that you can wear to be with animals, basically. But the color still flows through that.

DRUIG

SSD: Druig is like a monk. He thinks deeply about everything. So his costume is very dark, a monastic shape, 'cause it's quite long. But it's very strong in the center. And there's no complication about his look. It's very linear. And then, as we go through time with him, he just gets darker and darker.

MAKKARI

SSD: Makkari is the runner. She's super quick — she speed-reads and everything. When we get to the modern world, we gave her this slightly 1970s/super-modern feel of jeans and a tee shirt. She's just kind of easy within herself and actually just waiting to go home, basically.

KINGO

SSD: Kingo is a fighter, and he's strong. He has a very fantastic kind of silhouette. And as we go through time with him, he becomes more and more aware of himself in terms of his place. So, he goes from this kind of amazing, strong silhouette in his Super Hero suit, to the modern world where he's this sort of Bollywood superstar. We gave him kind of really expensive stuff that's like easy clothing, but we tailor it and [add] super expensive trainers. And he's got a jacket with a big "K" embroidered on the back, with a dragon.

PHASTOS

SSD: Phastos is the scientist, and he's a thinker too. So he's got that slightly monastic feel about him. Brian Tyree Henry was amazing to dress actually, 'cause he loves clothes. He just adored it all. And when we get to the modern world, we decided to make him kind of funky, layered looks with jeans and stuff, but still keep that slightly fitted, slightly monastic feel about everything, all the textures in the fabrics and stuff.

THENA

SSD: Thena's a warrior. She's strong. But equally, there's also a fragility about her. She starts off as this amazing gold goddess, and then slowly, through time, the gold sheds away. As we get through the periods towards the modern world, she becomes this fragile, almost damaged butterfly in a way, because she gets lost in her mind. And that's a very strong journey with her.

GILGAMESH

SSD: Gilgamesh is the strongest warrior. He's like a protector of Thena, particularly. They've been living in a place for a long time, so they don't change their clothes to the modern world. So, [their look] stops at about 1900. He has very old-looking clothes.

SPRITE

SSD: Sprite is an ancient person [who appears to be a] child. So, her colors are sort of teals and jades and silvers. And when we get to the modern world, we decided to give her this kind of Oliver Twist–type thing, but bring it into today rather than turn of the previous century. So, she kind of likes wearing men's trousers and waistcoats and shirts. And it's kind of slightly off the wall, and a bit grown up, but not.

SOUTH
AMERICA

A CLOSEUP LOOK AT SOME OF THE INTRICATE COSTUMES CREATED FOR THE MOVIE.

Producers Nate Moore and Mitch Bell talk about what it takes to bring a movie like *Eternals* to the big screen.

PUTTING IT TOGETHER

"It's definitely the biggest ensemble cast we've ever had for a first film..." – Nate Moore

Where did you draw the inspiration for Eternals*?*
Nate Moore (Executive Producer): In looking for new properties, we obviously comb through the history of Marvel comics. And *The Eternals* is a title that has popped up in a lot of different conversations. But the expectation, I think, by our fans, is that we're really gonna mine from Neil Gaiman's early 2000s run. But for us, the true inspiration was from Jack Kirby's original 1976 run. And that is partially because he really did steep that in sort of a world history, the history of the Aztecs. A lot of his design language, even his narrative inspiration was from the history of the world. We thought that was just a palette we hadn't seen before.

What was the casting process like?
NM: It's definitely the biggest ensemble cast we've ever had for a first film. I think the last time we even attempted to build a cast that size was *Guardians of the Galaxy*. And what is interesting about the Eternals, even narratively, is that the Celestials and the Eternals wanted to recruit a group of people who could integrate themselves on Earth. And the truth about Earth, is that there's people from all walks of life. There's people who look different from each other. There's people of all ages. And that allowed us to build a cast of a lot of talented people that aren't all from the same place. So, in almost every respect, this is our most international cast. There are five men, five women. And that's all part of the narrative of why the Eternals came here and why they built their team the way they did. And it allowed us to work with a lot of talented people, like Angelina Jolie, Gemma Chan, Richard Madden, younger actors like Lia McHugh or Barry Keoghan, up-and-coming actors like Brian Tyree Henry or Lauren Ridloff, and a very popular actor from South Korea named Don Lee. Salma Hayek, who can forget her? We really got to play with a lot of super-talented people who had never met each other. But they did find so many things in common that they became a family off-screen almost more quickly than they did on-screen. We don't always have a lot of time for rehearsals. But we did on this movie. So, a lot of the cast got to hang out here in Pinewood Studios in London before we ever rolled cameras, which I think translated to a different dynamic on set because they really knew and liked each other. And I think that really informs how they played the characters.

ABOVE: GEMMA CHAN AS SERSI, COLLABORATING WITH CHLOÉ ZHAO.

ABOVE: RICHARD MADDEN AND GEMMA CHAN WITH VICTORIA ALONSO (EXECUTIVE PRODUCER).

What are the challenges of putting together a film of this size and scope?

NM: Part of it is, you don't have a road map. Whenever you launch a first film, it's building that aesthetic so that it does stand alone, whether that be *Doctor Strange* or *Ant-Man* or *Black Panther*. So much work is done up front to try and build out a world that feels like its own world. Our filmmaker, Chloé Zhao, who comes out of a more naturalistic style of filmmaking, really pressed us to try and figure out how to shoot more of this on practical locations. This is a film that takes place outside and out of the blue screen more than anything we've tried before. Which again is challenging not just from a logistical standpoint of getting your crew to different places, of finding places where you can shoot outside, of battling rain and the elements, but also to shoot footage that then you can put this sci-fi overlay onto it in a way that is successful is challenging. It's hard on your crew. It's hard on your cast. It's hard on our visual effects team, and postproduction will be a challenge for that reason, too. But it's all in service of an aesthetic that's totally different. And, again, that's a challenge we wanted to take on, because after 25 some-odd movies, you have to be willing to push the envelope. And our audiences are ready to take that jump with us.

What is it about this comic book series that excited you in the first place?

Mitch Bell (VP, Physical Production, Producer): It's always the basis where it starts, [in this case] with Jack Kirby. The great thing about *Eternals* that I love, is the fact that it spans through time. I love the fact that we can go through history and check in with Super Heroes. Because in all of our movies so far, all we've seen in terms of historical Super Heroes is Captain America [*Captain America: The First Avenger*] in World War II. So, to me, this is awesome, 'cause we can see them at the dawn of mankind. How were they in Mesopotamia? How were they in Babylon? Where are they during the middle centuries? So, I think that the exciting part of this is truly that, it's the history of the Super Heroes.

What do you think director Chloé Zhao brings to the table?

MB: It's interesting, because Chloé has such a good take on this [property]. And [it was obvious] when she pitched the idea, she knows these characters. She knows what she wants, and she understands the Eternals. She knows them. She knows what she's doing. She understands the time span. I think that the great thing is, whenever you talk about it, she knows exactly what she wants to do. Every day, she walks in with her storyboards there that she writes herself, that she draws herself, and knows what we want to do on that day. So, I think it couldn't be in better hands.

What journey do you hope audiences go on?

MB: For Marvel Studios, and this is what I always say, if I can leave a theater happy and excited, it's a win, right? So, I think that for this film, you'll have both those things. You'll get the epicness of this, you'll feel the scope and the scale. You'll feel the historical impact. And you're getting introduced to ten new Super Heroes in the Marvel Cinematic Universe. Who doesn't want to see that?

ABOVE: RICHARD MADDEN AS IKARIS, CHLOÉ ZHAO, AND ANGELINA JOLIE AS THENA WHILE DISCUSSING A SCENE.

FILMING THE CELESTIAL.

Writers Matthew and Ryan Firpo tell us what it was like to write a unique set of characters like Sersi, Ikaris, and company.

FROM PAGE TO SCREEN

"I think you can expect a lot of fun out of this movie, but at the same time, an exploration of a lot of very serious philosophical themes..." – Ryan Firpo

This movie seems quite different from other Super Hero films. Can you talk about that?
Matthew Firpo (writer): At its heart, *Eternals* is an epic. It has this incredible, diverse cast of characters and heroes. And for us, it's really exciting to be telling a love story. We have this amazing canvas, and it's something that they've never been able to do before in the Marvel Cinematic Universe by having these sort of immortal, ancient aliens. We basically look at the scope of human history and the way that these characters have sort of been there across time. And it's really given us an opportunity to tell a story that we've never seen before in the Marvel Cinematic Universe.

Ryan Firpo (writer): I think *Eternals* is unique because it's an epic story that takes place over the course of 7,000 years. And, at its heart, it's a love story, a romance between the two main characters, Sersei and Ikaris, which we haven't seen in a Marvel movie before. We've seen romance, but we haven't seen it as the central driving force of a movie like it is here.

How would you describe the tone of the film?
RF: I think the tone is a little bit more serious perhaps than we've seen in Marvel movies before. We also do some fun things where we kind of play with actual historical events through human history and tie those into the story of the Eternals. I think you can expect a lot of fun out of this movie, but at the same time, an exploration of a lot of very serious philosophical themes that revolve around what it means to be human.

ABOVE: SERSI AND IKARIS SHARE A QUIET MOMENT TOGETHER.

MF: *Eternals* is about immortality. It's about a love story. It's about identity. It's about duty, and we're exploring all these things that so many amazing Super Heroes have done before but specifically we're looking at it over the course of the entirety of mankind's history here on Earth.

We know the Celestials figure in this movie. Can you talk a little about them?

MF: We're really excited to explore the origins of, essentially, the entire Marvel Cinematic Universe in our film. We're looking at maybe, for the first time, meeting Celestials face-to-face that you've sort of seen glimpses of in other films. But, what we're really doing is exploring the origins of this universe, of these characters, of this planet and of powers. So, ultimately, the film is a human story about universal stuff like love and duty and honor.

What do you think makes the Eternals unique among Marvel Super Heroes?

MF: We're really excited about *Marvel Studios' Eternals* because they're this incredible diverse cast of heroes who are all shapes and colors and sizes. And really, it's the first time we've ever been here on Earth where we've had a team of Super Heroes that really are as diverse as Earth itself, as humanity is. What *Guardians of the Galaxy* did so well, was bringing this really fantastic band of misfits together and exploring family and what that meant. And with *Eternals*, we're really looking at the bonds of family through duty, through purpose, over the course of 7,000 years.

RF: I think the other thing I'll add is that the Eternals are unique in that all their powers are not about offense. They're not just about fighting. Their purpose, at its core, was to help humanity develop and expand and evolve. Not all the Eternals are fighters. All of them can fight, but a lot of their powers are centered around helping humanity grow.

What kind of an impact do you think this movie will have on the Marvel Cinematic Universe?

MF: We think — we hope — *Eternals* is going to change everything you know about the MCU. We're sort of exploring its absolute Celestial origins. We're looking forward out into cosmic space and really, we're looking at the whole way that the MCU has worked in the past and trying to reinvent it and sort of create a new context for where all these heroes are going to go.

ABOVE FROM LEFT: KINGO, SERSI, AND SPRITE FACING THE ENEMIES.

THENA PREPARING FOR THE BATTLE.

8-04

THE CAST AND CREW ENJOY A LIGHTER MOMENT DURING THE SHOOT.

MARVEL STUDIOS LIBRARY

MOVIE SPECIALS

- **MARVEL STUDIOS' *SPIDER-MAN FAR FROM HOME***
- **MARVEL STUDIOS' *ANT-MAN AND THE WASP***
- **MARVEL STUDIOS' *AVENGERS: ENDGAME***
- **MARVEL STUDIOS' *AVENGERS: INFINITY WAR***
- **MARVEL STUDIOS' *BLACK PANTHER* (COMPANION)**
- **MARVEL STUDIOS' *BLACK WIDOW***
- **MARVEL STUDIOS' *CAPTAIN MARVEL***
- **MARVEL STUDIOS: THE FIRST TEN YEARS**
- **MARVEL STUDIOS' *THOR: RAGNAROK***
- **MARVEL STUDIOS' *AVENGERS*: AN INSIDER'S GUIDE TO THE *AVENGERS*' FILMS**
- **MARVEL STUDIOS' *AVENGERS*: AN INSIDER'S GUIDE TO THE *AVENGERS*' FILMS**

MARVEL STUDIOS' BLACK WIDOW: **THE OFFICIAL MOVIE SPECIAL**

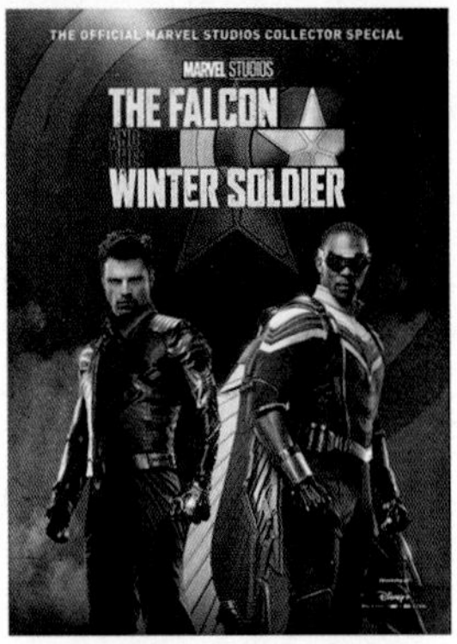

MARVEL STUDIOS' THE FALCON AND THE WINTER SOLDIER: **THE OFFICIAL MARVEL STUDIOS COLLECTOR SPECIAL**

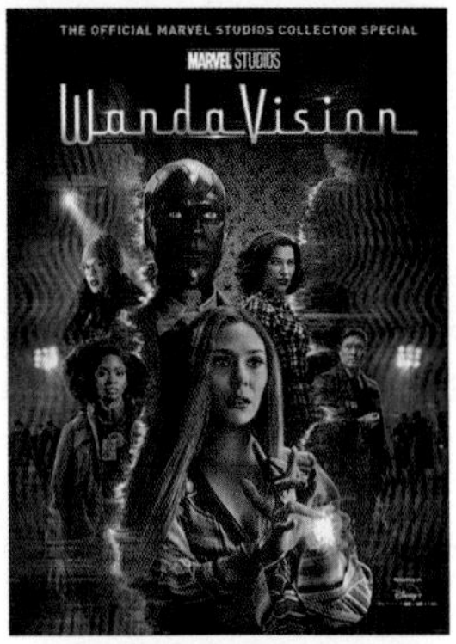

MARVEL STUDIOS' WANDAVISION **THE OFFICIAL MARVEL STUDIOS COLLECTOR SPECIAL**

STAR WARS LIBRARY

STAR WARS: THE EMPIRE STRIKES BACK: **THE 40TH ANNIVERSARY SPECIAL EDITION**

STAR WARS: THE MANDALORIAN **GUIDE TO SEASON ONE**

STAR WARS INSIDER: **THE FICTION COLLECTION VOLUME 2**

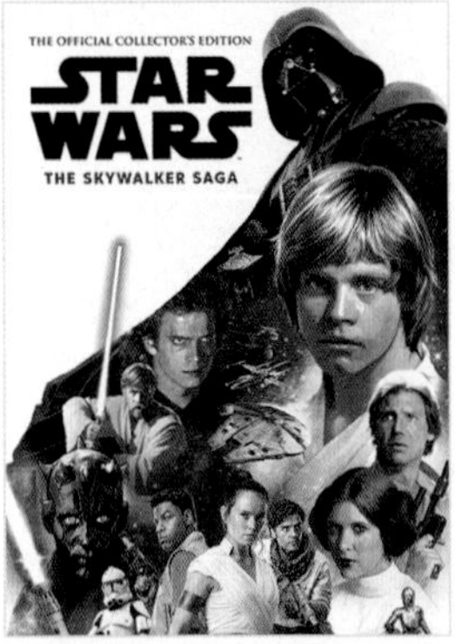

STAR WARS: THE SKYWALKER SAGA **THE OFFICIAL COLLECTOR'S EDITION**

- ***ROGUE ONE: A STAR WARS STORY*** THE OFFICIAL COLLECTOR'S EDITION
- ***ROGUE ONE: A STAR WARS STORY*** THE OFFICIAL MISSION DEBRIEF
- ***STAR WARS: THE LAST JEDI*** THE OFFICIAL COLLECTOR'S EDITION
- ***STAR WARS: THE LAST JEDI*** THE OFFICIAL MOVIE COMPANION
- ***STAR WARS: THE LAST JEDI*** THE ULTIMATE GUIDE
- ***SOLO: A STAR WARS STORY*** THE OFFICIAL COLLECTOR'S EDITION
- ***SOLO: A STAR WARS STORY*** THE ULTIMATE GUIDE
- **THE BEST OF *STAR WARS INSIDER*** VOLUME 1
- **THE BEST OF *STAR WARS INSIDER*** VOLUME 2
- **THE BEST OF *STAR WARS INSIDER*** VOLUME 3
- **THE BEST OF *STAR WARS INSIDER*** VOLUME 4
- ***STAR WARS*:** LORDS OF THE SITH
- ***STAR WARS*:** HEROES OF THE FORCE
- ***STAR WARS*:** ICONS OF THE GALAXY
- ***STAR WARS*:** THE SAGA BEGINS
- ***STAR WARS*** THE ORIGINAL TRILOGY
- ***STAR WARS*:** ROGUES, SCOUNDRELS AND BOUNTY HUNTERS
- ***STAR WARS*:** CREATURES, ALIENS,AND DROIDS
- ***STAR WARS: THE RISE OF SKYWALKER*** THE OFFICIAL COLLECTOR'S EDITION
- ***STAR WARS: THE MANDALORIAN*:** GUIDE TO SEASON ONE
- ***STAR WARS: THE EMPIRE STRIKES BACK*** THE 40TH ANNIVERSARY SPECIAL EDITION
- ***STAR WARS: AGE OF RESISTANCE*** THE OFFICIAL COLLECTORS' EDITION
- ***STAR WARS: THE SKYWALKER SAGA*** THE OFFICIAL COLLECTOR'S EDITION
- ***STAR WARS INSIDER: FICTION COLLECTION*** VOLUME 1
- ***STAR WARS INSIDER: FICTION COLLECTION*** VOLUME 2

MARVEL LEGACY LIBRARY

MARVEL CLASSIC NOVELS

- **WOLVERINE** WEAPON X OMNIBUS
- **SPIDER-MAN** THE DARKEST HOURS OMNIBUS
- **SPIDER-MAN** THE VENOM FACTOR OMNIBUS
- **X-MEN AND THE AVENGERS** GAMMA QUEST OMNIBUS
- **X-MEN** MUTANT EMPIRE OMNIBUS

NOVELS

- **MARVEL'S GUARDIANS OF THE GALAXY** NO GUTS, NO GLORY
- **SPIDER-MAN MILES MORALES** WINGS OF FURY
- **MORBIUS** THE LIVING VAMPIRE: BLOOD TIES
- **ANT-MAN** NATURAL ENEMY
- **AVENGERS** EVERYBODY WANTS TO RULE THE WORLD
- **AVENGERS** INFINITY
- **BLACK PANTHER** WHO IS THE BLACK PANTHER?
- **CAPTAIN AMERICA** DARK DESIGNS
- **CAPTAIN MARVEL** LIBERATION RUN
- **CIVIL WAR**
- **DEADPOOL** PAWS
- **SPIDER-MAN** FOREVER YOUNG
- **SPIDER-MAN** KRAVEN'S LAST HUNT
- **THANOS** DEATH SENTENCE
- **VENOM** LETHAL PROTECTOR
- **X-MEN** DAYS OF FUTURE PAST

THE GUARDIANS OF THE GALAXY **THE ART OF THE GAME**

***MARVEL'S AVENGERS BLACK PANTHER: WAR FOR WAKANDA*:** **THE ART OF THE EXPANSION**

MARVEL'S *CAPTAIN AMERICA: THE FIRST 80 YEARS*

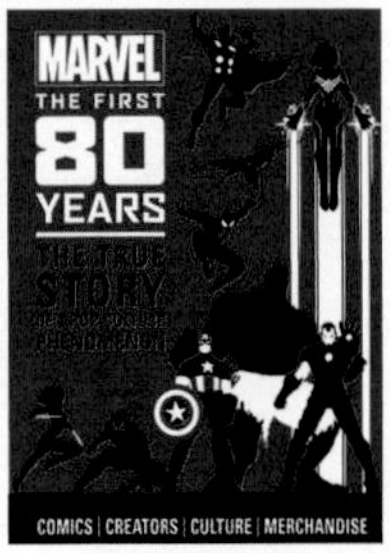

MARVEL: *THE FIRST 80 YEARS*

- **X-MEN** THE DARK PHOENIX SAGA
- **SPIDER-MAN** HOSTILE TAKEOVER

ART BOOKS

- ***THE GUARDIANS OF THE GALAXY*** THE ART OF THE GAME
- **MARVEL'S *AVENGERS*: *BLACK PANTHER: WAR FOR WAKANDA*** THE ART OF THE EXPANSION
- **MARVEL'S *SPIDER-MAN MILES MORALES*** THE ART OF THE GAME
- **MARVEL'S *AVENGERS*** THE ART OF THE GAME
- **MARVEL'S *SPIDER-MAN*** THE ART OF THE GAME
- **MARVEL *CONTEST OF CHAMPIONS*** THE ART OF THE BATTLEREALM
- ***SPIDER-MAN: INTO THE SPIDER-VERSE*** THE ART OF THE MOVIE
- **THE ART OF IRON MAN** THE ART OF THE MOVIE

AVAILABLE AT ALL GOOD BOOKSTORES AND ONLINE

TITAN-COMICS.COM | **TITAN**BOOKS.COM